The Safe Nanny Handbook

EVERYTHING
YOU NEED TO KNOW
TO HAVE PEACE OF MIND
WHEN YOUR CHILD
IS IN SOMEONE ELSE'S CARE

PEGGY ROBIN

QUILL
WILLIAM MORROW
New York

To Kathy, Fiona, Christine, and Liz,
with appreciation and admiration for everything you have done
for my children

While this book is intended to give you a general overview
of the issues involved in hiring a nanny, it is not intended
as a substitute for personalized legal advice. Families may
wish to consult their own legal advisers prior to making any
employment decision.

Library of Congress Cataloging-in-Publication Data

Robin, Peggy.
The safe nanny handbook : everything you need to know to have peace of mind
while your child is in someone else's care / [Peggy Robin].—1st ed.
p.   cm.
Includes index.
ISBN 0-688-16214-2
1. Nannies—United States.   2. Nanny placement agencies—United States.
I. Title.
HQ778.5.R63   1998
649'.1—dc21   98-23462
CIP

Printed in the United States of America

First Edition

1 2 3 4 5 6 7 8 9 10

BOOK DESIGN BY CATHRYN S. AISON

www.williammorrow.com

✳ ACKNOWLEDGMENTS ✳

Because I relied so heavily on those I interviewed for information, advice, research materials, and ideas, I owe my first thanks to all the parents and nannies who took time out of their busy schedules to talk to me or respond to my E-mail survey. Most were content to remain anonymous, but I do want to credit by name several of the professionals in the field who gave me the benefit of their expertise. Fiona Klinefelter, of EF Au Pair (and a former full-time nanny), was a fountain of information about the workings of the Au Pair program and how it is different from the nanny care option. Christine Maniscalco, operator of an on-line nanny support group and creator of the Life with Nanny Web Site, not only provided valuable advice and interesting anecdotes, but she also put me in contact with other nanny and parenting sources, and steered me in the right direction in finding knowledgeable people to interview. Richard Eisenberg of Eisenberg & Associates Insurance Agency supplied facts and figures about health insurance options for nannies and employers; Valerie Gatzionis of the "Search Your Nanny's Past" division of Search & Locate Unlimited Investigative Services answered my many questions about the scope and cost of privately investigating a potential employee's background.

Rebecca Goodhart was a helpful and patient editor at William Morrow. Bill Adler, Jr., as he has done with my five previous books, came through with research, kept my E-mail up and running, and was an expert navigator of the World Wide Web. Bill Adler, Sr., came up with the idea for this book and encouraged me all the way through. Gloria Adler steadily kept an eye out for relevant articles and information and faithfully supplied me with clippings.

Most important, thanks are due to my own children's nanny, Kathryn Burke, who made it possible for me to do my work every day in peace and quiet and with the absolute assurance that my children were in safe and loving hands.

�֎ CONTENTS ✷

CHAPTER THREE
Hiring Independently

57

The Downside of Agencies • Running Your Own Search—It Doesn't
Have to Be Intimidating • Step One: Decide What You're
Looking For • Step Two: Think About Where to Find the Nanny
You Want to Hire • Step Three: What Your Notice or
Advertisement Should Say • Step Four: Prescreen Your Applicants •
Steps Five, Six, and Seven: Covered in Chapter Four
• Step Eight: Check Her Records

CHAPTER FOUR
Interviewing and Reference Checking

81

The Interview • Stage One: Face-to-Face Talk (Adults Only) •
Stage Two: The House Walk-Through • Stage Three: Meeting Your
Child(ren) • The Reference-Checking Telephone Call • Stage Four:
The Follow-up Interview • The Driving Test (Optional) •
Two Cardinal Rules for All Employers of Nannies

CHAPTER FIVE
Hiring and Firing

107

Making Your Choice • Making the Offer • Negotiating Pay and
Benefits • Negotiating Duties • Three Non-Negotiable Issues •
Negotiating the Live-in Agreement • Procedures During the First
Two Weeks • Video Surveillance • Firing

CHAPTER SIX
Toward a Long-term Relationship

134

Show Respect for the Job She Does • Communicate Effectively •
Build a Friendship • Better Living with a Live-in • Watch Out for
the Little Green Monster! (Jealousy) • Servant Culture Nannies •
Party Girls

THERE ARE GOOD NANNIES
OUT THERE

It's an Awesome Responsibility

𝒩othing is more precious to you than your child (or your children) and so nothing is more important than your child's safety and well-being. That means when you leave your child with someone during your working day, you want to be sure that the person you've chosen can be trusted to take good care of your child.

The question is: How do you know? Can you ever *really* be sure?

Most working parents appreciate the high level of caution they need to bring to the choice of a caregiver. Most understand that it's an awesome responsibility. We also know with frightening clarity what can happen to our children if we choose less than wisely—though we seldom like to think about such things.

There are times, however, when the subject becomes all but unavoidable. When the news of the day is dominated by the death of a child and the arrest of the caregiver for murder, parents' worst fears come to the fore. Public debates rage not just over the guilt or innocence of the accused, but over the larger question: Are children safe with hired caregivers? Few cases have stirred up as much controversy as that of a British au pair Louise Woodward. Practically every working parent is familiar with at least the outlines of the case: On February 4, 1997, the eighteen-year-old was left at home with a toddler and eight-month-old baby Matthew Eappen, while the parents, both doctors, went to work. Later that day the parents were summoned to the hospital and told their baby was in a coma. The doctors who examined him have concluded that he was a victim of "shaken impact syndrome." As they later testified in court, injuries of the sort that killed Matthew Eappen typically occur when a baby is slammed headfirst against a hard surface and then shaken violently for several minutes. Despite her consistent denial that she did anything wrong, Louise Woodward was convicted of first-degree murder (although the presiding judge subsequently reduced the conviction to involuntary manslaughter and freed her from prison after the nine months she had served awaiting trial).

During the trial and for months afterward the TV, radio, and newspapers were full of voices arguing over a wide range of legal issues. Was the charge of first-degree murder warranted? Did the prosecution unfairly withhold evidence from the defense? Did the judge have the power to overturn the original verdict? While the media were filled with voices discussing these abstract points of justice, for many of the working parents who followed the case the main point was not in the least abstract—it was agonizingly close to home:

"How can I be sure I never have such a person looking after *my* kids?"

Just as the airwaves were full of pundits offering their wisdom on the legalities involved, there was no shortage of experts in child development and psychology who came forward to give worried parents advice about the childcare issues raised. Not just experts, but people from all walks of life, wanted to weigh in on the question. Radio and TV call-in shows reported their second highest volume of calls over the case (second only to the O. J. Simpson trial in terms of public response).

An oft-heard opinion, issued by certain experts as well as by a large percentage of laypeople, was that there *is* no way to be sure that a child's caregiver is safe. If the parents truly put their child's welfare first (so said many talk-show callers, so wrote many newspaper letter-writers) then one parent needs to stay home to make sure of it. The stay-at-home parent (callers either said explicitly or implied) should be the mother.

For most of us working parents, hearing such advice only adds to our agonized reaction to the case. There is no question, for the vast majority of us, that we will continue to hold down jobs in the workforce. Sixty percent of mothers of children six and under are already employed on a full-time basis. According to a poll in *USA Today*, even if their families could get along on a single income, the majority of working mothers (55 percent) would not give up their jobs.

Since the reality is that most mothers have accepted a dual role (for getting things done both on the job and in the home), there is no alternative for us except to rely on some form of childcare. The question is not "Should we?" but "*How* do we?" What causes such horror and doubt is that we look at the Eappen family and can easily see ourselves in their places. We find ourselves wondering "What would I have done if Louise Woodward had shown up for an interview at *my* house?" It was easy to picture her as she must have seemed to the hiring couple—sitting there, sweet-faced, soft-spoken—and she had been agency-screened, to boot. We have to ask ourselves, "Wouldn't I have hired her, too?"

Now, of course, with the twenty-twenty vision that comes with hindsight, it is not difficult to point to things the Eappens did wrong. (See the list beginning on page 4.) Still, without experience in hiring and without a time-tested screening process, almost any couple might have done the same. So, of course, we're frightened. If the facts of the case were not frightening enough by themselves, there was the near-constant media hype that seemed to incite panic. Tabloid headlines like "KILLER NANNY!" were enough to make a working mom want to bolt out of the office, run home, and stand guard over her child twenty-four hours a day.

Still, we know we need to keep our heads and our jobs. The problem of safe childcare is serious, but it is not unsolvable. There *are* good nannies out there. I state this categorically, because I've had four good nannies myself. You probably know some families, too, who have had nannies they have trusted and loved—and even if you don't, undoubtedly you have seen children out on the playground, in the library, or at the grocery store in the company of an excellent caregiver.

Employers of good nannies are the logical ones to answer the question "How do you go about finding safe childcare?" That's the approach I took when I accepted the assignment to write this book. I sought out parents and asked them for their best ideas and advice.

Without exception the parents I contacted agreed to be interviewed, happy to pass along the practical tips and techniques that most of them had simply stumbled upon in the course of their many hiring experiences. They were also quick to tell me all those things that they'd done wrong in the days before they found their best nannies. You can learn from the bad just as well as the good, of course, and it is my sincere hope that with the help of this book, all this learning will come from your reading and not from your own hard-taught experience.

Twelve Important Lessons You Can Learn from the Louise Woodward Case

1. *When you find yourself seriously dissatisfied,* fire the nanny!

Louise Woodward's employers were unhappy with her almost from the start. As they later testified in court, she seemed more interested in the nightlife around Boston and in partying with her friends than in looking after the children. However, rather than start searching for a new and better nanny, the parents hoped by means of stricter written rules to keep her focused on her job. All that did, apparently, was to increase her resentment and unhappiness. You *never* want your children left in the care of someone you know is angry at you.

2. *Never let your course of action be dictated by your agreement with an agency.*

By tying themselves to an agency, with its hefty fee and its complicated rules governing the replacement of a fired caregiver, the Eappens accepted limitations on their employment options. If they fired Louise, their choices were either (a) take a chance on another live-in caregiver from the same agency that sent them Louise Woodward or (b) go outside the agency to hire afresh, but lose their nonrefundable fee. In such a situation it was not surprising that they chose to try to work with what they had and get some return on their investment. However, when it comes to decisions about safe childcare, parents need to put any thought of money spent out of their minds, and base their actions exclusively on their evaluation of the caregiver's ability to do the job well.

3. *Always remember you are an employer, not a foster parent.*

If your childcare provider is acting like a child herself (she's an unruly teenager, rebelling, staying out to all hours, drinking with false ID, showing up late for work, and otherwise testing the limits of your authority), it is not your job to help her grow up. Your job is to do what's in the best interest of your child, and that means not leaving an immature person in charge. Resist the urge to listen to the caregiver's excuses or give a second chance. The surest way for her to learn from her behavior is to lose her job. The surest way to protect your children is to see that she doesn't learn important life lessons at their expense.

4. *Do a trial run before hiring.*

You need to have a very good idea *before* the person starts to work for you how she will function on the job with your children. Interviewing and reference checking provide important clues to her character, but the clearest way to get the full picture is to see her in action. Make time for a few weekend or evening working sessions with your children, while you remain in the house to observe. That way you have the best chance to spot problems before either of you makes a commitment to the job.

5. *Don't hire an au pair to do a nanny's job.*

There are few teenagers up to the task of watching an infant and a toddler for a ten-hour day. The U.S. government's au pair program (described on page 15 in Chapter One) was created primarily as a cultural exchange program, permitting young adults from overseas to experience a year in this country at low cost. *Au pairs are not childcare professionals,* and families who are seeking full-time childcare professionals should be aware that an au pair may not be mature enough to cope with the stresses and strains of normal infant care on a full-time basis.

6. *Allow yourself enough time to search for the very best candidate.*

When someone who seems so-so applies for the position, and no one better has come along to be interviewed, it's often tempting to give in to time pressure and take what's available now. That may be fine for hiring a lawn-care service or a house cleaner, but when it comes to childcare, a different rule applies. In a period yielding lackluster interviewees, it may be necessary for the parents (and this means the father as well as the mother) to alter their work schedules in order to provide childcare themselves until a first-rate candidate can be found. That is preferable to leaving a child with a person, even for a day, in whom you have less than complete confidence.

7. *Practice emergency procedures.*

Louise Woodward's own testimony reveals how poorly trained she was to handle an emergency. By her own account, she wasted precious minutes looking up the parents' pager numbers (which she had not bothered to memorize) and trying to page them several times each, prior to dialing 911. Any person in charge of a child in a critical situation must know that you always call for medical help first.

8. *Stay in close touch with the caregiver of an infant.*

For children under two it's a good idea for one or both parents to call in once or twice during the day, just to be kept up on what the baby is doing. When all is well, these daily calls will provide brief reassurances that the baby is fine and at the same time will serve to keep the lines of communication between parent and caregiver flowing freely. A parent should not have to hear a whole day's report on baby's activities packed into a few rushed minutes at the end of the workday. In their regular phone contacts, the parents should listen carefully for any signals that the caregiver sounds harried, frustrated, annoyed, resentful, or overwhelmed, and take any follow-up action that may be needed, including firing.

9. *Avoid being influenced by appearances.*

Psychologists have designed studies proving that most people make many assumptions about behavior based on looks. There is a natural human tendency, whenever we are introduced to someone with a sweet face and a quiet, respectful demeanor, to assume that the person must be gentle, caring, and kind. Louise Woodward's demure appearance almost certainly influenced the Eappens' decision to hire her and to keep her on, even after problems began to surface. We just need to keep reminding ourselves of the old truism, "Looks can be deceiving."

10. *Avoid being influenced by national stereotypes.*

The Disney movie *Mary Poppins* has almost certainly led many of us to form the image of the English nanny as the perfect caregiver for children. (See the section headed "On the Delicate Subject of National Stereotypes" in Chapter One for more examples of the ill effects of this phenomenon.)

11. *Be alert for signs of unsuitability.*

Unless you're hiring someone you've already known for years, you'll need to keep a close watch on your new nanny for the first few weeks, with antennae tuned to signals that she's not up to the job. It came out during testimony at the trial that Louise Woodward particularly disliked certain aspects of infant care, and that she considered changing dirty diapers a gross and disgusting chore. If the Eappens had picked up on her attitude during her first few weeks of work, they might have decided to replace her with a caregiver who had more of an affinity for the specific tasks required.

12. *Choose live-out care over live-in.*

There is no question that live-out childcare offers the parents greater safety and flexibility than live-in. Changing caregivers, for one thing, becomes far easier when you don't have the complication of getting the old nanny out of your house so that the new one can move in. Lifestyle clashes are far less apt to affect your employment relationship if all you need to concern yourself with is the nanny's on-the-job performance. The Eappens testified at the trial that when Louise Woodward was angry at them, she would not come out of her room until the precise start of her workday. When the living situation is so fraught with tension that the caregiver can barely stand being around the house, how can she possibly be trusted to love and protect your children?

What This Book Will Cover

Hiring a nanny involves a fair number of skills and procedures, which may make it seem daunting at first. But taken one step at a time, each part of the process is really quite doable. This book will address in chapter-by-chapter sequence each of the points below:

- the kind of childcare you need (An easy-to-take quiz will help you evaluate your childcare options.)
- where to begin your search
- how to work with an agency to find a nanny
- how to hire a nanny on your own
- how to interview and check references and background
- how to negotiate insurance, vacations, sick days, and other benefits
- how to write an employment agreement and a live-in agreement
- how to evaluate the nanny's performance during the trial period
- how to train your nanny to be as safety conscious as you are yourself (a room-by-room safety guide around the house and in other places)
- how to solve problems that may arise in the nanny-employer relationship (a question-and-answer chapter)

How This Book Was Researched

I had no difficulty finding parents who were willing to talk about their hiring experiences. My neighborhood in Washington, D.C., is made up mainly of two-career families, who use one form of childcare or another, with nannies as the most common option. Of the immediate eight neighboring houses, six of us employ nannies. To reach beyond a single neighborhood I also posted a few notices in likely locations, such as local preschools, toy stores, and pediatricians' offices, looking for parents to interview on the subject. From the local Washington, D.C., and suburban vicinities I interviewed a total of fifty-five parents and thirty-one nannies.

Just to be sure that the experiences of those I interviewed in person were not atypical of families in the rest of the country, I also sought contact with parents and nannies through the medium of the Internet. After posting a query on five different parenting discussion groups, I began receiving E-mail responses from many different states. Some of the respondents simply answered a list of questions that I had posted on-line. Others provided their telephone numbers, and I conducted a fifteen- to twenty-minute phone interview with those respondents. In all, I made contact with sixty-two parents and twenty nannies.

Although I firmly believe that parents and nannies with real-life experience have the most to contribute by way of practical suggestions, I did not ignore the experts. I consulted books in print by child development experts, heads of nanny agencies, and others with professional childcare credentials.

Not surprisingly, I discovered that there is no broad consensus on what's the best childcare choice for children. Some experts conclude that a licensed, well-staffed day-care center is the answer for most working parents; others favor nanny care. A hiring guide written by an agency director would naturally come out strongly for hiring only through a reputable agency. Then there are books that argue against using any form of childcare whatsoever. The authors cite studies purporting to show that children of stay-at-home mothers do better across the board (by tests measuring emotional, intellectual, and social development) than children who spend their day with hired help. Then there were studies that showed just the opposite: that children of well-educated, dual-career families, who spent their days in a stimulating environment (regardless of whether that setting was established by a nanny or a day-care operator) did as well as children whose mothers stayed home.

If you are interested in the theoretical aspects of the childcare question, you will probably enjoy reading a book by psychology professor Diane E. Eyer called *Motherguilt* (Times Books, 1996). Dr. Eyer examines the forces of history and culture that have shaped common American attitudes toward childcare (or rather, *against* childcare) and contributed to the widespread sense among working mothers that, by seeking careers, they are somehow shortchanging their children.

For those who already have confidence that working outside the home is the right choice, the debate is moot. You want to know the who, what, where, when, and how of getting your child the best quality of care when you are not at home. That's what I asked of the parents and nannies I interviewed. Not being a social scientist, I do not pretend to have done any sort of statistical or sociological analysis of their answers. I simply collected their stories and extracted from them any useful suggestions, warnings, and ideas I believed to be helpful for readers of this book. I urge you to keep in mind that families are not all alike, and that what works well for one family might not be so wonderful for another. You need to pick and choose what you think will work for *you*.

You may also want to know something about how my own experience as an employer of nannies has influenced my attitudes. The section that follows provides a brief summary of my background as an employer of nannies and other childcare providers.

Personal Experience

My husband and I have had in our employ a total of nine regular caregivers in our home during the past seven and half years, starting from when our first child was three months old. We have liked most of them, disliked two (and fired both of them promptly), and loved four of them, including the one we have now.

We have had all types, acquired in all the different ways. One nanny came to us through a high-priced nanny agency. The rest of the full-time nannies we hired independently, by means of newspaper ads or notices posted on bulletin boards. In the early days, we hired part-time college students, whom we recruited through the job placement centers of various local colleges. We have had American girls from the Midwest, the West Coast, the East Coast, and the South. We have had foreign-born ones as well: one Trinidadian; one Irish nanny; and our current one, who is English. They have all been live-out, except for one nanny, who in the process of relocating to accept our job offer, stayed in our basement until she could move into her own apartment (which we found and provided for her, rent-free).

Our best nannies have stayed for more than two years; our worst ones were let go within weeks. One time I fired a nanny on the same day she started work, having realized almost from the moment that she stepped inside the door that it had been a mistake to make her an offer.

Four of our nannies have been far more than employees—they became friends, and to my children each has been much like a third parent. My children's love for their nannies has been intense, which has meant, among other things, that it has been *very* hard on them each time one of our long-term nannies has had to say good-bye. But we have always made a point to stay in touch, and we feel these women will always be a part of our lives.

Our first long-term nanny, Lizzie, was a part-time college student, who left us when she graduated. She moved back to her home state of Pennsylvania to become a kindergarten teacher. Our second, Christine, was our first full-time professional nanny (she was the one hired through an agency). While she worked for us during the day, in the evenings she took graduate courses in education. After two years with us she earned her M.A., and, as had been her plan from the start, she left us to become a full-time high school teacher. She now works at an excellent Washington area private school, and in her spare time runs her own tutoring service. Although she has few weekends or evenings free these days, she still baby-sits for us when the timing can be work out.

Our third nanny, Fiona, came from Ireland, where she had been a ballet teacher. Before she found us, she had worked for two other families under less than happy circumstances. Her first employer had a failing business and was constantly fending off creditors, leaving Fiona with instructions to lie to bill collectors and angry customers over the phone. In the end, the employer was unable to pay for Fiona's time, and she had to leave. Her second family insisted she live in, but then could not provide a suitable live-in space, moving her "temporarily" into their dining room on a cot. With no doors to close, no privacy was possible. She informed the family that she would not stay long under such conditions, and three months later, when she saw our advertisement, she quit. Our whole family benefited from her devoted care for two and a half years, until she married an international labor lawyer, and needed to adjust her schedule to accommodate her husband's high-powered career. Reluctantly, we both concluded that she needed a job with more flexible hours. She is now the regional coordinator for an au pair agency. Though she travels a lot, she still visits our children as often as she can, and we generally arrange for her to stay overnight with them whenever my husband and I go out of town together.

Our current nanny is Kathy. We found her through what I now realize is the most reliable source of nannies—"The Nanny Network" (described in Chapter Three). Fiona had many connections with nannies all over the area, and immediately upon telling us that she would be leaving, started spreading the word up and down the network that her job would soon be available. A friend of a friend of a friend led us to Kathy, who has been with us ever since. We love her, our children love her, and we are secure in the knowledge that our love is returned.

When you have a nanny like this, you truly have peace of mind.

When I'm in my office working on a book, I feel not a speck of guilt about leaving my children in another's care, because it's clear to me that my nanny does the job every bit as well as I do. Well, I hate to admit it, but in some ways, maybe better! When I come home to find my girls working so carefully and patiently with Kathy's help at an art project I could never have organized, I find myself feeling grateful, not guilty, for all the richness she has added to their lives. When you have a good nanny, your children get more of a good thing (nurturing)—not less.

It is my hope that with the help of this book you will be able to get to the same point. Of course, you know that there's always a bit of luck involved—but you realize, too, that you can learn to recognize good luck when it hits you. And more important, you learn to watch out for the signs that a bad situation is developing and know when and how to bail out.

Yes, you'll take more time and put in more effort than you would if you were to take the first okay candidate who came your way. But you know your children deserve nothing less than the very best care you can find.

If this book makes it easier for you to end up with your own Lizzie, Christine, Fiona, or Kathy, then I will know my time spent away in my office, with my kids in their nanny's care, has been very well spent.

NANNY FACTOID:
THE NANNY WHO BECAME A PRINCESS

Lady Diana was a nanny for an American family in London before she became engaged to Prince Charles. After Diana's death, the parents who had employed her were interviewed. They said she was a wonderful nanny, very attached to their young son, and she kept up the connection long after she had moved on to her royal life, coming to visit the family wherever she made a tour that included their hometown in Boston. They knew from personal experience what a loving and generous spirit the world had lost.

❊ C H A P T E R O N E ❊

DO YOU NEED A NANNY?

Who Is a Nanny (and Who Is Not)?

*P*arents these days have many different types of childcare to choose from. Not all childcare providers are nannies—although some people use the term too broadly, calling anyone hired to look after children a nanny. During the Louise Woodward case, the media regularly referred to the defendant as such (she wasn't; she was an au pair). The first order of business then is to have a clear set of definitions. The most commonly used forms of childcare are (going roughly in order from least expensive to most expensive):

- day-care center
- family day care
- au pair
- shared nanny
- housekeeper (with childcare responsibilities)
- nanny

Each of these will be described briefly. I have based my write-ups not on the dictionary definitions of the terms but on the everyday usage of the childcare professionals I interviewed for this book. One of the first questions I always asked of anyone who supervised children was "What do you call yourself?" My second question asked her to explain what distinguished her role from other forms of childcare.

A **day-care center** is a childcare facility run by a director. It may be large or small, but it will generally have at least ten children, divided by age groups, each group supervised by a few staff members. Concerning the level of staff training, qualifications, and safety procedures, much depends on the regulatory and licensing requirements of the state. Day-care centers may also set many rules and practices on their own. For example, some day-care centers accept infants under three months; others do not. Parents usually contract for care for a certain number of hours per month. The center makes arrangements for substitute caregivers when staff members are sick or on vacation, so that there are no gaps in coverage.

In **family day care**, children are cared for in the home of the caregiver. Depending on the state and local law, the caregivers may be licensed and held to strict standards for staffing, space, and hygiene, or they may operate entirely unregulated, or any variation in between. A typical family day-care arrangement might be one of a mother with her own children in school looking after the children of two different families (let's say, an infant and a toddler) in her own home. She might also accept additional older children in her home in an after-school program. She could be the sole caregiver, or rely on full-time or part-time assistants. Usually if she is sick or unavailable, she will arrange for a substitute, so that care is continuous.

A **babysitter** or **mother's helper** is a young woman (usually) who looks after children part-time, for an hourly wage, and with no special training. She may be hired on an as-needed basis (for an evening, say, or a weekend day), or she may work on a regular weekly schedule. The term "mother's helper" is generally used when the sitter works under the supervision of a stay-at-home mother, and the arrangement is most common when the child is a newborn or infant under a year old. The mother's helper may leave many of the childcare duties to the mother, while taking over other chores such as grocery shopping, helping out in the kitchen, and straightening up the house. Although both terms suggest a short-term and/or part-time employee, a family could cover their full-time childcare needs by means of two or even three part-time caregivers (the box on page 17 gives an example). With a large enough pool of part-timers to draw from, a family could even have a good chance of finding a substitute in the event of the scheduled sitter's illness.

A **shared nanny** looks after the children of two or occasionally three families. She may work entirely in one family's house, or alternate weekly, or move between houses according to some other mutually worked-out schedule. The hiring families must reach an agreement on all aspects of the job—not just whom to hire, but how to split her wages between them, how much vacation time she will receive, and when she will take it, and all other benefits and duties that make up her employment package. Sharing need not be simultaneous: A common arrangement puts the nanny in one family's home during the morning (caring, for example, for an infant whose mother has a part-time job in the afternoon), and then has her go to school to pick up the older children of another family, whom she will look after from three to six-thirty. Each set of parents in the shared nanny arrangement may work out the ratio of pay and time allotment that best suits the parties involved.

An **au pair** is a young person who comes to America from a foreign country as part of an official exchange program managed by the U.S. Information Agency. Au pairs are subject to a multitude of regulations laid down in legislation by the U.S. Congress. These young adults, usually women, must be between the ages of eighteen and twenty-six, stay for no more than one year, work no more than forty-five hours a week, and be provided with room and board, plus a stipend that is currently set at $230 per week (full-time). Because the program was created primarily as an avenue of cultural exchange, the au pair is required to further her education in this country by taking classes. Her relationship with the family is meant to be like that of an older daughter (the term *au pair* in French actually means "on par," or "as an equal"). Her child-care chores should not be much greater than what one would expect of a visiting relative from overseas. *The program was not set up to function as a source of cheap labor.* Despite explicit language on this point in the enabling legislation, au pair agencies often advertise themselves to parents as the "affordable alternative" in childcare. As a consequence, it is not surprising that many parents get the impression that an au pair is basically a younger and less expensive version of a professional nanny.

A **housekeeper/nanny** is a full-time employee working for just one family, but her duties include more than just taking care of children. Much of her time is spent cleaning the house. She seldom has any formal training in childcare. Housekeepers typically will view their position as more of a servant to the family than as one with significant impact on the upbringing and development of the children. It is not unusual for the person occupying this position to be poorly educated, an immigrant from a third-world country, with limited fluency in English. However, one also finds housekeepers who make up in practical experience and common sense what they lack in formal education— and this may be especially true for older women who have successfully brought up their own children or even grandchildren.

A **nanny** is a full-time childcare provider who works in the employer's home. She may live there as well, or she may have her own residence. She may be a graduate of a nanny training program or she may have taken courses in childcare, first aid, and other skills though a community college, adult education center, or other institution. She may intend to remain a nanny throughout her working life, or she may be working as a nanny for a limited time, with a goal to eventually work toward an advanced degree in some other child-centered field such as a teaching, pediatric nursing, child psychology, or special needs therapy or counseling. She views her work as a profession and will not usually accept non-child-related household tasks. (For example: A nanny will do the children's laundry, but not the general household wash; she will prepare lunch for the children, but will not cook and serve the family's breakfast; she will help a child change the litter in the gerbil's cage in the child's room, but she will not clean the fish tank in the father's study.) A nanny will usually vacation with the family, but she will be paid for her time, and later in the year, enjoy a separate, paid vacation on her own. If she falls ill or becomes unavailable for any reason, it is usually up to the parents to arrange for their children's care until she can return to work.

Nannies Are Not for Everyone

Why has so much space been given to describe other forms of childcare when the focus of this book is on finding and keeping a good,

FULL-TIME WITH PART-TIMERS

Joan is a minister who has three children under eight. She is often at home with her kids during the normal work week, but on Sundays she is always busy at her church. She needs forty hours a week of childcare. Here's how she worked it out with the use of three part-time sitters. Tina, a college student, sits all day Sunday. Joan has Mondays and Tuesdays off. On Wednesday and Friday afternoons, a part-time nursery school teacher named Linda looks after the children. On Wednesday and Friday mornings, as well as all day Thursday, a nursing student named Debbie is the sitter. Although Joan frequently works on Saturdays, putting last-minute touches on her sermon and overseeing church activities, Joan's husband is the primary caregiver for the day.

safe nanny? *Because nannies are not for everyone.* When families who are not well suited to the nanny-employer relationship take one on regardless, the safety factor drops dramatically and a risky situation may develop. (Later in this chapter there will be a quiz you can take to find out if nanny-care is the best childcare option for your unique circumstances.)

The box on pages 18–19 tells the story of two families who hired nannies when nanny-care was not the most suitable choice. If those parents only had the opportunity to take the quiz on pages 26–30, they would have realized ahead of time that a nanny would not be able to give them the kind of overtime coverage they needed. Unfortunately, too many families never perform any kind of analysis of their childcare needs. They view nannies as the most prestigious choice, and then simply assume that prestige equals safety and high quality. In a neighborhood in which most of the parents employ nannies, a family may not even consider any of the other options. The results of such thoughtless hiring may be seen on any city playground on any working day, as children are left to run wild, barely supervised, while supposedly under the care of a hastily hired, underpaid, and unqualified servant who has been given the title of "nanny."

The chart on pages 19–23 presents an easy-to-follow format concerning the main advantages and disadvantages of each of the forms of childcare you may want to consider. The quiz on pages 26–30 will help you to analyze your own situation, to see if a nanny is the right choice for your family's way of life.

"A NANNY WAS THE WRONG CHOICE FOR US" (TWO STORIES WITH THE SAME CONCLUSION)

The Dooney family was not in a position to pay the salary of a qualified, well-trained nanny. Instead of researching other options, they continued their search until they found Susie, who was young, eager, and sweet—and willing to work for half the expected salary of an older, experienced nanny. It took the parents about a month to see that Susie wasn't even worth the low wage she received. The first time a child was sick with a cold, she panicked and called for both parents to come home. They also discovered that she had no sense of priorities: She would leave the baby screaming in his crib for twenty minutes while she went to fold the laundry. One day she called the mother at work and said she just had to leave—there was a family emergency and she had to go home and deal with it. It turned out that she'd had a fight with her boyfriend the night before, and he'd called her the next day and asked her to meet him to make up. The Dooneys told her not to come back. By then it was clear to them that it was time to rethink their choices. Their "bargain" nanny was costing them more in hassle and worry than she was saving them in salary. They could see that they would be better off with a higher-quality provider of a less expensive form of childcare, and so they began to explore their other options. They ended up finding a well-run family day-care situation, where their child has been happy ever since.

Money wasn't the issue for the Allen family. For the mother, a conference planner, and the father, a tax lawyer, time was the real problem. When it was tax season or when a major conference was coming up, it was impossible for one parent or the other to miss a day of work. It just so happened that the

Allen's old nanny became seriously ill in the middle of a high-pressure period for both. They found themselves without a caregiver, with no time to interview replacements, and no possibility of either one staying home to train and supervise a new nanny—if they were lucky enough to find one. So they called an agency and just grabbed the first candidate they were sent. They guessed from the start that hiring Jenny was a mistake, but they supposed they could hang on for the next two months or so—just until the rush season was over. In that time she got into, not one, but *two* car accidents (though, fortunately, for the Allens, no one was hurt); she left kitchen knives out on the counter, and once she left the house with the teakettle on a lit burner (and the fire department had to be called to blow out all of the resultant smoke with a high-powered fan).

"Never again!" the Allens vowed, as they let Jenny go. Their two- and four-year-old girls are now doing just fine in a carefully managed day-care center half a block away from both parents' downtown offices—and this way, even in rush periods, one parent or the other can usually manage to stop in to see the kids at lunch.

SEVEN CHILDCARE OPTIONS: A COMPARISON CHART

FACTORS TO CONSIDER	DAY-CARE CENTER	FAMILY DAY CARE	BABYSITTER OR MOTHER'S HELPER	SHARED NANNY	AU PAIR	HOUSE-KEEPER/NANNY	NANNY
COST* (See note at end of chart for explanation)	LOW TO MID PRICE RANGE	LOW TO MID PRICE RANGE	LOW TO MID PRICE RANGE	MID RANGE	MID RANGE	MID TO HIGH PRICE RANGE	MID TO HIGH PRICE RANGE
HOURS	FULL WORK WEEK; OVERTIME USUALLY AVAILABLE AT HIGHER PRICE	FULL WORK WEEK, OVERTIME MIGHT NOT BE AVAILABLE	USUALLY A PART-TIME ARRANGEMENT (2 OR MORE SITTERS MAY PROVIDE FULL-TIME AND POSSIBLY OVERTIME)	FULL WORK WEEK, OVERTIME MAY BE DIFFICULT TO ARRANGE	45 HOURS PER WEEK IS MAXIMUM ALLOWED UNDER CURRENT LEGISLATION	FULL WORK WEEK; ADDITIONAL HOURS MAY BE PART OF JOB OR ARRANGED AT HIGHER COST	FULL WORK WEEK, ADDITIONAL HOURS MAY BE PART OF JOB OR ARRANGED AT HIGHER COST

FACTORS TO CONSIDER	DAY-CARE CENTER	FAMILY DAY CARE	BABYSITTER OR MOTHER'S HELPER	SHARED NANNY	AU PAIR	HOUSE-KEEPER/ NANNY	NANNY
IF CARE-GIVER IS ILL . . .	HAS SUBSTI-TUTES AVAILABLE—NO DISRUP-TION IN CARE	MAY HAVE SUBSTITUTES AVAILABLE—DEPENDS ON HOW FAMILY DAY CARE IS SET UP	UP TO PAR-ENTS TO ARRANGE SUBSTITUTE CARE	UP TO PAR-ENTS TO ARRANGE SUBSTITUTE CARE	UP TO PAR-ENTS TO AR-RANGE SUBSTITUTE CARE	UP TO PAR-ENTS TO ARRANGE SUBSTITUTE CARE	UP TO PAR-ENTS TO ARRANGE SUBSTITUTE CARE
CONTINU-ITY OF CAREGIVER	STAFF TURN-OVER MAY BE HIGH, NEED TO CHECK CENTER'S RECORDS	USUALLY GOOD CHANCE FOR SAME CARE-GIVER OVER LONG TERM	PART-TIME SITTERS TEND TO CHANGE SITUATIONS MORE OFTEN THAN FULL-TIMERS	HINGES ON PLANS OF THE SHARING FAMILY AS MUCH AS ON CAREGIVER	LIMITED BY AU PAIR LEG-ISLATION TO ONE YEAR PER AU PAIR	PROSPECTS GOOD FOR LONG-TERM CARE BY SAME PERSON	PROSPECTS GOOD FOR LONG-TERM CARE BY SAME PERSON
INDIVIDUAL ATTENTION TO YOUR CHILD(REN)	NO, BUT GOOD FAMILY DAY CARE HAS HIGH STAFF TO CHILDREN RATIO	NO, BUT GOOD FAMILY DAY CARE HAS HIGH STAFF TO CHIL-DREN RATIO	YES, AL-THOUGH PART-TIMERS MAY HAVE COM-PETING RE-SPONSIBILITIES FROM OTHER JOBS	NO—TIME IS SPLIT CAR-ING FOR CHILD OR CHILDREN OF SHARING FAMILY	YES	YES, AL-THOUGH RE-SPONSIBILITY FOR HOUSE-HOLD CHORES WILL REQUIRE SOME ATTENTION	YES
EXPERIENCE OF CAREGIVER	VARIES GREATLY FROM CENTER TO CENTER	VARIES GREATLY DE-PENDING ON INDIVIDU-ALS AT FAMILY DAY CARE	PART-TIMERS ARE USU-ALLY YOUNG AND LESS EX-PERIENCED THAN FULL-TIME CHILDCARE PROVIDERS	SHOULD BE ABLE TO FIND A SHARED NANNY WITH MANY YEARS OF EXPERIENCE	DUE TO YOUTH OF AU PAIRS IN PROGRAM, FEW WILL HAVE MANY YEARS OF FULL-TIME CHILDCARE EXPERIENCE	MAY HAVE MORE CLEANING EXP. THAN CHILDCARE EXP.; NEED TO INVESTI-GATE THOROUGHLY	SHOULD BE ABLE TO FIND NANNY WITH MANY YEARS OF EXPERIENCE
QUALIFICA-TIONS AND TRAINING	VARIES, DE-PENDS ON LOCAL REGULATIONS	VARIES, DE-PENDS ON LOCAL REGULATIONS	SELDOM RE-CEIVE FOR-MAL TRAINING	SOME MAY HAVE PASSED SAFELY AND/OR CHILDCARE COURSES	AU PAIR PROGRAM INCLUDES A BRIEF CHILDCARE/ SAFETY COURSE	HOUSE-KEEPER MAY NOT HAVE SPECIFIC CHILDCARE/ SAFETY TRAINING	MANY PRO-FESSIONAL NANNIES HAVE CHILDCARE AND SAFETY TRAINING AND/OR ARE COLLEGE GRADS
PARENTS ABILITY TO SET RULES, DETERMINE SCHEDULE	RULES AND HOURS SET BY CENTER	MAY WORK WITH PAR-ENTS TO SET RULES AND SCHEDULES	PARENTS SET RULES AND SCHEDULE	SHARING FAMILY MUST AGREE ON RULES AND SCHEDULES	RULES/ SCHEDULE MUST FIT WITHIN WEEKLY LIMITS OF AU PAIR PROGRAM	PARENTS SET RULES AND SCHEDULES	PARENTS SET RULES AND SCHEDULES

FACTORS TO CONSIDER	DAY-CARE CENTER	FAMILY DAY CARE	BABYSITTER OR MOTHER'S HELPER	SHARED NANNY	AU PAIR	HOUSE-KEEPER/ NANNY	NANNY
CARE FOR INFANTS, ABILITY TO WORK WITH BREAST-FEEDING MOTHER	FEW ACCEPT INFANTS UNDER 3 MONTHS; MAY NOT DEAL WITH FROZEN BREAST MILK, MAY PROHIBIT BREAST-FEEDING VISITS	MAY NOT ACCEPT INFANTS UNDER 3 MONTHS; MAY SET RULES ABOUT BREAST MILK, BREAST-FEEDING VISITS	MAY NOT BE QUALIFIED TO CARE FOR INFANT UNDER 3 MONTHS OR DEAL WITH BREAST MILK IN A HYGIENIC MANNER	MAY SET OWN RULES REGARDING INFANTS UNDER 3 MONTHS AND BREAST-FEEDING VIS-ITS OR STOR-AGE OF BREAST MILK	AU PAIR PROGRAM SETS RE-STRICTIONS ON CARE OF NEWBORNS	PARENTS NEED TO DETERMINE HOUSE-KEEPER'S QUALIFICA-TIONS TO DEAL WITH VERY YOUNG INFANT AND HANDLE BREAST MILK PROPERLY	EXPECT QUALIFIED PROFES-SIONAL NANNY TO BE CAPABLE OF DEALING WITH INFANTS UNDER 3 MONTHS AND HAN-DLE BREAST MILK PROPERLY
OVERNIGHT CARE AVAILABLE	NO	NOT USUALLY	NOT USUALLY	NOT USUALLY	POSSIBLY, WITH AN OLDER, WELL-TRAINED AU PAIR	POSSIBLY, WITH A WELL-TRAINED, EXPERIENCED HOUSE-KEEPER/ NANNY	YES, MOST PROFES-SIONAL NANNIES EXPECT TO RUN HOUSEHOLD WHILE BOTH PARENTS ARE AWAY
TRAVEL WITH FAMILY	NO	NO	CAN SOME-TIMES BE WORKED OUT	SELDOM CAN BE WORKED OUT (UN-LESS SHAR-ING FAMILY TAKES SAME VACATION)	YES, OFTEN EXPECTED BY AU PAIR	CAN SOME-TIMES BE WORKED OUT	YES, TRAVEL WITH FAM-ILY IS OFTEN MADE PART OF THE CON-DITIONS OF EMPLOYMENT
CONVEN-IENCE	DEPENDS HOW CLOSE DAY-CARE CENTER IS TO HOME OR WORK	DEPENDS HOW CLOSE FAMILY DAY CARE IS TO HOME OR WORK	IN-HOME CONVENIENCE	DEPENDS ON LOCATION WORKED OUT IN SHARING ARRANGEMENT	IN-HOME CONVENIENCE	IN-HOME CONVENIENCE	IN-HOME CONVENIENCE
HEALTH AND HY-GIENE CONCERNS	HIGHEST RATES OF COLD, FLU, EAR INFEC-TION, DIAR-RHEA AND LICE—NOT FOR CHIL-DREN WITH COMPRO-MISED IM-MUNE SYSTEM	COLD, FLU, EAR INFEC-TION, DIAR-RHEA AND LICE RATES HIGHER THAN FOR CHILDREN WITH SOLE CAREGIVERS	IF SITTER HAS OTHER CHILDCARE JOBS, MAY INCREASE EXPOSURE TO INFEC-TIOUS AGENTS	SHARING WITH OTHER FAMILY IN-CREASES CHANCE FOR COLDS, FLUS, EAR INFEC-TIONS, DI-ARRHEA, AND LICE	NO IN-CREASED RISK	NO IN-CREASED RISK	RISK IS LOW-EST WITH NANNY PROFESSION-ALLY TRAINED IN HYGIENIC PRACTICES

FACTORS TO CONSIDER	DAY-CARE CENTER	FAMILY DAY CARE	BABYSITTER OR MOTHER'S HELPER	SHARED NANNY	AU PAIR	HOUSE-KEEPER/ NANNY	NANNY
CARE FOR SICK CHILD	SICK CHILD USUALLY MUST STAY HOME	SICK CHILD USUALLY MUST STAY HOME	WILL CARE FOR SICK CHILD	DEPENDS ON RULES WORKED OUT WITH NANNY AND THE SHARING FAMILY	WILL CARE FOR SICK CHILD	WILL CARE FOR SICK CHILD	USUALLY TRAINED TO CARE FOR SICK CHILD
CARE FOR CHILD WITH SPECIAL NEEDS	MAY NOT ACCEPT SPECIAL NEEDS CHILD	MAY NOT ACCEPT SPECIAL NEEDS CHILD	MAY NOT BE TRAINED TO WORK WITH SPECIAL NEEDS CHILD	MAY NOT ACCEPT SPECIAL NEEDS CHILD	PROBABLY NOT CAPABLE OF WORKING WITH SPECIAL NEEDS CHILD	PROBABLY NOT CAPABLE OF WORKING WITH SPECIAL NEEDS CHILD	CAN HIRE NANNY SPECIALLY TRAINED TO WORK WITH SPECIAL NEEDS CHILD
EASE OF HIRING	MAY NEED TO WAIT FOR OPENING OR START OF SESSION	MAY NEED TO WAIT FOR OPENING	HIRING PROCESS DETERMINED BY PARENTS, MAY BE VERY SIMPLE	TIMING AND OTHER HIRING DECISIONS MUST BE WORKED OUT WITH SHARING FAMILY	HIRING INVOLVES COMPLETING APPLICATION PROCESS, SCREENING, AS SET BY AU PAIR AGENCY	HIRING PROCESS DETERMINED BY PARENTS, MAY BE VERY SIMPLE	HIRING PROCESS DETERMINED BY PARENTS— THOUGH GOOD NANNY IN HIGH DEMAND MAY NEGOTIATE TERMS
EASE OF CHANGING CAREGIVER	IF REQUIRED TO PAY FEES FAR IN ADVANCE, MAY LOSE MONEY WHEN CHANGING CAREGIVERS	IF REQUIRED TO PAY FEES FAR IN ADVANCE, MAY LOSE MONEY WHEN CHANGING CAREGIVERS	USUALLY EASY TO CHANGE CAREGIVER	DEPENDS ON TERMS OF AGREEMENT ENTERED INTO UPON HIRING	REPLACEMENT POLICY DETERMINED BY AU PAIR AGENCY; HEFTY FEES MAY BE SACRIFICED IF CHANGE IS MADE WITHOUT AGENCY APPROVAL	USUALLY EASY TO CHANGE CAREGIVER; (IF AGENCY INVOLVED, MAY BE COMPLICATED)	USUALLY EASY TO CHANGE CAREGIVER, BUT MAY BE COMPLICATED BY AGENCY INVOLVEMENT, OR RULES SET AT TIMES OF HIRE; PROFESSIONAL NANNY USUALLY GIVEN ADVANCE NOTICE AND SEVERANCE PAY
DRIVING/ TAKING CARE OF ERRANDS	NO	NO	POSSIBLY (YOUNG SITTERS MAY HAVE LIMITED DRIVING EXPERIENCE)	POSSIBLY— DEPENDS ON AGREEMENT WORKED OUT BY ALL PARTIES	POSSIBLY (YOUNG, FOREIGN AU PAIR MAY HAVE LIMITED EXPERIENCE WITH U.S. TRAFFIC CONDITIONS	POSSIBLY (NEED TO CHECK DRIVING RECORD CAREFULLY)	GOOD DRIVING RECORD USUALLY EXPECTED OF PROFESSIONAL NANNY

FACTORS TO CONSIDER	DAY-CARE CENTER	FAMILY DAY CARE	BABYSITTER OR MOTHER'S HELPER	SHARED NANNY	AU PAIR	HOUSEKEEPER/ NANNY	NANNY
SOCIALIZATION	GOOD OPPORTUNITY FOR CHILD TO LEARN SOCIAL SKILLS	GOOD OPPORTUNITY FOR CHILD TO LEARN SOCIAL SKILLS	MAY NOT SEEK OUT OPPORTUNITIES FOR CHILD TO BE WITH OTHER CHILDREN	GOOD OPPORTUNITY FOR CHILD TO LEARN SOCIAL SKILLS	AU PAIR MAY FEEL ISOLATED IN STRANGE COUNTRY, UNAWARE OF OPPORTUNITIES TO MEET OTHERS	HOUSEKEEPER MAY NOT HAVE TIME FOR OUTINGS DUE TO HOUSECLEANING DUTIES	PROFESSIONAL NANNY SEEKS OUT OPPORTUNITIES FOR CHILD TO LEARN SOCIAL SKILLS

*A Note About Cost and Other Factors in the Childcare Options Chart

Although affordability is one of the key issues determining the form of childcare you may choose, this chart does not provide dollar figures to define the price range. That is because there is simply too much variability from region to region to be taken into account. The salary of a top nanny in Birmingham, Alabama, for example, may be half that of her counterpart in Beverly Hills, California—though the skills, years of experience, and educational levels of the two nannies may be substantially the same. Furthermore, the top-level nanny in Los Angeles will probably expect (and quite possibly require) exclusive use of a car. In Manhattan, on the other hand, not only would a car be unnecessary, but in most cases the nanny would not even be asked to produce a driver's license.

Because no chart can adequately account for all the regional and local variations that go into determining the cost of childcare (and the qualifications you might expect at the varying levels of pay), each potential childcare employer should start out by doing a little investigation into the matter. The information you seek should be at hand within a phone call or two. First, look up the numbers of one or two well-known nanny agencies in your area. (If you don't know of any agencies, try the Yellow Pages of your telephone directory under "Childcare" or "Nanny.") Call and ask the agency's representative what is the minimum weekly salary that their nannies expect to receive; also ask what is the typical salary for the most qualified and experienced of their nannies. That gives you the range for nannies in your part of the country.

Remember, this amount is base pay. You should come up with an approximation for an additional amount to take into account what you will be spending for the nanny's taxes, health insurance, and room and board (if you are offering a live-in situation). The agency representative ought to be able to help you arrive at a realistic weekly dollar amount for those costs, too.

The agency's estimate of their lowest cost for a nanny per week gives you what on the Comparison Chart is "mid-range." The agency's estimate of the earnings of a nanny with the highest level of qualifications will define the "high range."

Figuring out what's at the lowest end of the low range is simple: It's the minimum wage. Even in high-cost parts of the country there are always some workers who cannot command more than the preset government minimum for their labor—either because they are unskilled, inexperienced, limited in their available hours, or lack working papers (illegal aliens).

Low-wage earners aren't *necessarily* low-quality. They just may not have had time to acquire the training or experience to allow them to sell their services at a better rate. If you have the time and ability to train a young person yourself (supervising closely until you are certain that she is up to the demands of the job on her own), you might do well with a nanny who will work for start-up pay. Just be sure to increase her salary as her skills improve, or you will be sure to lose her to a more generous employer!

Nannies Top the Chart (but Have Some Drawbacks, Too)

As you can see by a quick perusal of the categories on the chart, nannies are by almost every standard equal or superior to all the other childcare choices—except in the following three categories:

1. **Cost.** Nannies are without question the most expensive of the listed childcare choices.
2. **Substitution.** Nannies do not arrange for their own substitutes in the event of illness or absence for another reason.
3. **Overtime coverage.** Nannies may not be available to work extensive or unscheduled hours beyond their regular workday.

Any one of these three considerations may be important enough to rule out nanny-care for your family. If, for example, it would seriously strain your family's budget to pay a salary at or above the typical nanny's minimum requirement for your area, then you should be seriously exploring some or all of the five listed alternatives to nanny-care. Now suppose you are able to pay the going rate, but your job places demands on your time that a single childcare provider would have difficulty covering by herself. For example, let's say you are the sole crisis coordinator for your company's computer system, on call whenever the network goes down. On certain days without warning you will have to work till 8 P.M., or come in at the crack of dawn. While most nannies can accommodate unusual hours from time to time, an individual nanny—even a live-in—could not guarantee her availability in a crisis of long duration. Only a full-time, fully staffed day-care center may provide the assured level of coverage for a parent in such a demanding occupation—and the overtime fees that such a center would assess would be enough to bump the cost of that option out of the low- to mid-range typical of most day-care operations and into the mid- to high-range that is comparable to the cost of a full-time nanny.

The third problem—what to do when a caregiver is ill or otherwise unavailable—is one most working parents must confront. One parent or the other (usually the mom) has to take time off from work to make up for the caregiver's absence. For some of us (like me, a self-employed writer), it's possible to shift much of the work over to the children's nap times, and get the rest of the day's work done after they've gone to bed at night. It's an inconvenience for a few days, until the nanny comes back. But for many parents no such flexibility is feasible. When both parents are under pressure from work to come in every day, it makes sense for them to choose a form of childcare that comes with its own backup. By choosing a day-care center or a family day-care provider with staff assistants, parents need not fear consequences to their careers due to a caregiver's illness.

Is a Nanny the Right Childcare Choice for You?
A Self-Evaluation Quiz

Makeup of Family

For each child under one year of age, score 3 points.

For each child between the ages of one and three but not in preschool or any other daily program, score 3 points.

For each child between the ages of two and five enrolled in a preschool or other daily program on a part-time basis (twenty-four hours/week or less), score 2 points.

For each child between the ages of four and eleven in school full time (twenty-five hours/week or more), score 1 point.

For each child twelve or older, score 0 points.

For any child with a significant physical impairment (e.g., blindness, deafness, cerebral palsy), add 6 points.

For any child with a chronic condition requiring medication or other special care (e.g., diabetes, asthma, epilepsy, hyperactivity, attention deficit disorder), add 5 points.

For triplets or higher order multiples, add 5 points.

For twins, add 3 points.

In the case of parents separated, divorced, or never married, with primary custody to the person taking this quiz, add 5 points.

Parents' Workload

I work:

0–20 hours/week score 0 points

21–35 hours/week score 1 point

36–45 hours/week score 2 points

45+ hours/week score –4 points

My spouse works:

0–20 hours/week score 0 points

21–35 hours/week score 1 point

36–45 hours/week score 2 points

45+ hours/week score –4 points

My hours are unpredictable, but it's not unusual for me to work over 10 hours on any given day.

Score –4 for self

My spouse's hours are unpredictable, but it's not unusual for my spouse to work over 10 hours on any given day.

Score –4 for spouse

Childcare Budget

I have looked into the costs of the various childcare options in my area, analyzed my total household income, and have concluded that I can afford to pay:

in the high range, without strain on my budget	score 5 points
in the mid-range, without strain on my budget	score 1 point
in the mid-range, with some strain on my budget	score –1 point
in the low- to mid-range, with some strain on my budget	score –5 points
in the low range only	score –8 points

Travel

My spouse and I will be away together requiring overnight childcare one to three nights per year.	score 4 points

My spouse and I will be away together requiring overnight childcare four or more nights per year.	score 6 points
Either my spouse or I will be away from home separately, over four nights per year.	score 2 points per traveling spouse
My family will travel together on at least one vacation per year and would like to have childcare on the trip.	score 3 points

Driving and Errands

Looking after my children entails:

driving them places regularly	score 2 points
pet care	score 1 point
grocery shopping	score 1 point
preparing lunch daily for at least one child	score 1 point
preparing dinner daily for at least one child	score 1 point

Working Conditions and Benefits

Score points as indicated for each of the working conditions or benefits listed below that you are willing and able to provide:

housing, either live-in or rent-paid live-out	score 3 points
with own bathroom	add 1 point
with separate entrance	add 1 point
transportation	
nanny will have exclusive use of car	score 2 points
nanny will be allowed to borrow car for personal use	score 1 point
home very well served by public transportation	score 1 point

transportation will be left entirely up to nanny to arrange	score –3 points
health insurance	score 2 points
paid vacation time	score 1 point
paid sick days	score 1 point

Evaluating Your Score

21 points or greater

You could definitely benefit from having a nanny and are very likely able to provide a good employment situation for one. If you scored in this range but rated yourself at an income level that does not easily support a nanny's pay, then consider the suggestions offered in the section below titled "When Money is the Problem."

15 to 20 points

You could be in a borderline situation: There are some aspects of nanny-care that are right for your family, but there might be other childcare options that will suit you as well or better than nanny-care. If you scored in this range because of points subtracted for your long-working days or your unpredictable schedule, then you might consider looking for an extremely well-run day-care center that provides coverage for the overtime hours you frequently need. The high-powered dual-income couple for whom money is no object may achieve the same coverage by means of *two* full-time nannies, one for the 6 A.M. to 1 P.M. shift, the second for the 1 P.M. to 8 P.M. shift.

If you scored in this range because your children are older and need less than full-time supervision, you might consider using a part-time babysitter, an au pair, or a nanny shared with another family. Especially if you own a large house that needs a fair amount of cleaning and upkeep, consider taking on a live-in housekeeper who can keep an eye on the kids when they're home from school but who still will have time during their school hours to clean and cook.

14 points or fewer

A nanny probably isn't right for your family for a variety of reasons. Your children may not need a nanny's one-on-one care; her salary demands would perhaps be too great a strain on your budget; your schedule could be more intense than a single childcare provider can handle; or any combination of these. Keep exploring your options. Here's a suggestion for parents of school-age children, especially those old enough to be taking a foreign language—bring over an au pair who speaks the language your children are studying in school. This is exactly the situation for which an au pair is well suited. Since they are generally young and fun-loving, au pairs do best with children not so far away from their own age group. They are here as much to learn about their host family's way of life as they are to offer childcare. Children who are old enough to be interested in the au pair's country of origin and who can help introduce her to their own culture truly contribute to the idea of cultural exchange. For the family with little enthusiasm about helping to broaden the horizons of a young person from overseas, my advice is clear: Stick to childcare providers whose primary focus is their work.

A suggestion for those whose job schedule frequently or unpredictably requires more overtime than the typical nanny can provide: Find out what childcare arrangements your similarly situated co-workers are using. Perhaps there is a particular day-care center or family day-care provider that has worked out well for employees of your company. If there are enough of you struggling with the childcare issue, then you might even be able to band together, to establish (or induce your employer to establish) an on-site center that will handle your particular childcare needs.

Be creative, but above all, be careful as you investigate your choices!

When Money Is the Problem

Suppose a nanny suits you in every regard except the cost—is there anything you can do? Speaking from personal experience, I strongly recommend the shared-nanny option. You get many, if not most of the advantages of having your own nanny, but the costs are split in half. (Well, maybe not half, as a highly desirable nanny may be able to command a surcharge to cover the complications involved in looking after the children of two separate families.)

The chief drawback to this solution is the problem of finding a compatible nanny-share family. And what to do first: try to find the nanny and then look for the second family to split the bill? Or try to find a family that already has a good nanny and can share her time with you? Either one may work out for you—and sometimes the nanny herself can bring in a suitable share family and work out the details of the time and pay split for both.

You may also be able to use a professional share-nanny matching service. Of course, you must pay a fee for a successful match.

Nanny sharing can be set up entirely in your own home, entirely in the other family's home, or at alternating locations according to whatever schedule best suits the families. Good matches can be made in a variety of ways, as the examples below suggest:

- Parents of an only child seek another of a similar age and disposition, and the nanny looks after this nonbiological set of "twins."
- The parents of an infant may seek to share only with the parents of an older child, so that the nanny can devote the necessary greater attention to the baby. Usually the parents of the baby would be expected to pay a proportionately greater share of the salary as well.
- Two families can arrange for the nanny to work around their children's opposite school schedules. While the child of one family attends the morning session of a preschool, the nanny looks after the child of the other family. When the nanny goes to pick up the first child, she drops off the second child for the afternoon session, and has both children together only in the late afternoon.

Certain sharing situations are definitely to be avoided. Too many infants or toddlers in the same share situation may result in nanny overload. My rule would be to limit the number of children under age three to two per nanny—unless she works for the two different families at different times of the day.

Whatever the terms worked out by the sharing families, they should be spelled out in writing, each couple writing an Employment Agreement with the nanny, and then by a letter of understanding with each other.

Although it may take more time and effort to find the right players, with some necessary compromising along the way, parents whose hearts are truly set on the nanny-share option should (with a little creativity and flexibility on their part) be able to come up with a formula that works for them.

Live-in or Live-out?

This is one of the crucial issues you should certainly address before you begin your nanny search. If you don't have the space in your own home for a live-in, you may jump to the conclusion that the question is already decided, and that your only choice is live-out. That would be overlooking some options. Many families have managed to hire live-in help, despite lack of space in their own homes. Here are some of the solutions that have worked for others:

- Renting (or even buying) an efficiency apartment for the nanny to occupy in a building within walking distance of your home.
- Arranging with a neighbor to provide a room for the nanny in exchange for house-sitting, evening or weekend babysitting, or perhaps a nominal rent.
- Creating a new live-in space in your home. You may be able to finish off a basement or an attic room, convert a study or sewing room, turn a detached garage into a separate studio apartment, or use some other part of your house that had not, at first, sprung to mind. Just be sure the new room has enough light, ceiling height, and square footage to be habitable. You would be better off with a live-out nanny who is happy with her surroundings than with a live-in who is uncomfortable and resentful about being stuck in a broom closet.

CREATIVE SOLUTION FOR SMALL-BUSINESS OWNERS

Do you own a small business (consisting of perhaps yourself, your spouse, and three or fewer employees)? Consider offering a childcare benefit as part of your employment package. This will be greatly to your advantage if your other employees are young and unmarried and have no near-term prospects of having children. Since the IRS requires that benefits be offered equally to all employees of a company, you can create a benefit that only you and your spouse will be likely to need. Your nanny then becomes the company childcare provider and may be carried on your books as a company-paid employee, with all the benefits of an employee, such as health insurance and employment taxes, figured into your company's overhead. A big plus is that the paperwork for her withholding taxes and benefits will be handled by your company's bookkeeper or accountant.

Another way to structure the deal would be to have the company share childcare costs, paying an allowance per child that employees of the company may spend on their personal choice of childcare.

Even if you are currently self-employed, you may be able to take advantage of tax rules set up to encourage companies to provide a childcare benefit. Consult an accountant or a tax attorney to find out if it makes economic sense for you to give yourself a company name and operate as a small business. (You would then file Schedule C tax forms rather than report your income on the Schedule SE, the self-employment form). You may also want to look into the possibility of incorporating yourself. You would then become the sole employee of your corporation, and all your earnings would be gross corporate income, out of which you would pay yourself a salary and fund any benefits, such as a subsidy for childcare.

Always consult a knowledgeable financial advisor before restructuring your business or altering its tax status.

The question of livable space is by no means the sole determinant. Each family needs to consider a wide range of issues, assigning priorities in order of their importance to arrive at a decision that will lead to a safe and productive working situation for the nanny in their home.

No book can perform this calculation for you. However, the table on page 36 may help you to focus on those aspects of live-in or live-out childcare that are most important to you. It may be a useful exercise for you and your spouse to draw up separate lists, assigning points to each of the twenty qualities on the live-in/live-out table, in order of importance to each of you. Let's say, for example, that you place the highest priority on your privacy: Then give it 20 points. Let's say your spouse's number-one concern is overtime availability. He gives it 20 points. You give 19 points for ability to arrange vacations with the nanny; he gives 19 points to ability to change nannies easily, and so on down the list of advantages and disadvantages. You may even score some of the items on the list at 0—as would be the case with "parental jealousy" if you believe there is not the remotest possibility that your husband might feel attracted to a live-in. When you are done adding up all the factors, it should be readily apparent whether your greatest total is the sum of the live-in or live-out column of characteristics.

If you and your spouse take approximately the same view of your childcare needs, your two lists should be fairly well matched. However, if one of you leans strongly toward live-in and the other toward live-out, you should certainly try to work out your differences before you begin the hiring process. The table can also help to pinpoint just what the areas of disagreement are and so enable you to search for a creative solution that could serve the competing points of view. For example, if your spouse places highest priority on maintaining family privacy, but you give highest ranking to the convenient accessibility of a live-in, you and your spouse could work out a way to have a live-in but still, maintain some separateness of residence. Perhaps you have a detached garage you can convert into a one-bedroom cottage. Or you could approach a neighbor about renting out a basement room. You might seek out a widow or widower who lives alone in a too-large house, to work out an arrangement to provide housing for your nanny in exchange for a set amount of help around the house.

The key to a workable compromise is to listen to each other's opinions and treat each other's views with utmost respect and open-mindedness. It is far better to resolve the issue now, before you have someone living in your former study, than it is to have to argue about it in hushed whispers in the hall, as you're waiting for the nanny to vacate your now-shared bathroom.

As the final note, let me toss out my own personal take on the matter, based on my own experience as an employer of nannies and as an observer of many other employers and their live-ins: For the employer whose primary concern is safety, live-out is usually best. The main reason is that you are less encumbered when you want to make a change in a hurry. With a live-in, firing is nearly always complicated by the need to get the nanny out of your house. In an extreme case, she could even refuse to move out, and you'd end up having to start the eviction process. Anyone who has ever been a landlord can tell you that will be a nightmare.

Although many parents told of live-in nannies who became irreplaceable members of the family, for every one of these heartwarming tales there are perhaps two or three other stories about the live-in who "just didn't work out." Practically every employer of a live-in who spoke to me at some point made the analogy between finding the right live-in and choosing one's mate. It's generally not enough to find someone who is merely okay—you really need to fall in love with the person. Each one of us has his or her own little eccentricities and flaws, and you generally don't know what they'll turn out to be until after the person is under the same roof. If you love the person enough, you will put up with whatever those flaws may turn out to be. But if you don't love them, you may quickly find yourself growing irritated and tense, and can easily grow to dislike them (even as your children become more and more attached). If you're lucky, the feeling of wrongness of the match will be mutual, and you will be able to sever the connection without undue hostility. But if the relationship is lopsided and the live-in feels she is being unfairly discarded and dispossessed, then bringing about the end to the relationship may become as draining, emotionally and financially, as any divorce involving children.

Therefore, as with any serious commitment you make in life, do not rush in but be sure to give the matter your utmost care and due deliberation. If you choose wisely, you may indeed live happily ever after.

LIVE-IN VERSUS LIVE-OUT TABLE

ADVANTAGES OF LIVE-IN CHILDCARE	ADVANTAGES OF LIVE-OUT CHILDCARE
Convenience: The nanny does not have to travel to arrive at work.	**Privacy:** The family and the nanny do not intrude into each other's personal lives.
Overtime availability: The nanny will be much more likely to be able to work extra hours if she is right there.	**Fairness:** The family is less likely to try to take advantage of the nanny's proximity to get free overtime work out of her (leading to lower chances of nanny resentment and feelings of exploitation).
Fosters Intimacy: The nanny is much more likely to feel closely connected to the family if she lives with them and sees them in all aspects of their lives, not just during the workday.	**Reduces potential for parental jealousy:** Children are less likely to show more affection to the nanny than the parents (or the parents are less likely to *perceive* that to be the case) if the nanny goes back to her own family at the end of the workday.
Fosters commitment: If the nanny must move out of her home as well as look for a new job when she is considering changing jobs, she will be less likely to leave over trivial problems that could probably be worked out.	**Eases nanny changes:** Hiring a new nanny is made much more complicated when you have to arrange a housing switch at the same time. If you are intending to fire the old nanny, you will almost certainly have to tell her so well in advance, to give her a chance to find a new situation, while you openly begin your search for her replacement. This period will be fraught with conflicts.
Widens pool of available applicants: If you can offer live-in, you can still consider those who already have a place to live. Pool of applicants is effectively doubled.	**Allows you to select on basis of childcare abilities alone, not lifestyle:** You need not concern yourself with the nanny's taste in music, or romantic partners, or other personal preferences when her private time is fully her own.
Professionalism of nanny: The traditional professional nanny expects to be provided with room and board. Many of the best nanny agencies specialize in live-in nannies, so your chance of finding a highly qualified and experienced nanny are greater if you can offer a live-in situation.	**Decreases potential for jealousy over husband/nanny attraction:** Whether it is justified or not, a wife may feel anxious over the constant presence of an attractive young woman in her home. If that is the case, the emotional well-being of the family is probably better served by having the nanny maintain her own residence.
Prevents isolation: The nanny will feel more connected to the community and make friends more easily among other nannies if she lives with the family.	**Fosters businesslike relationship between employer and employee:** The parents need not involve themselves in fostering the nanny's social life; the nanny doesn't have to make adjustments to her social life to suit the sensibilities of her employers.
Savings for the family: If the family has a spare room to offer as part of the package, they probably can get a good nanny for a lower wage than they would need to offer to attract a good live-out nanny (provided that their spare room would otherwise not be income-generating space).	**Savings for the family:** If the nanny lives out, the family does not pay her board and other living expenses.
Savings for the nanny: She does not have to spend her own income on food or transportation.	**Greater income for the nanny:** Live-out nannies typically receive 25% to 40% more per week than live-ins. If she lives with her husband, parents, or some other rent-paying adult, she may not need to spend much (or any) of her own earnings on housing.
Vacation travel: The live-in is more likely to coordinate her vacation schedule with yours, and consider traveling with the family to be part of her job.	**Reduces likelihood of religious tension:** Since the live-out is at her own home on Christmas day, Easter Sunday, and other religious occasions, she is free to observe (or not observe) these and/or other holidays as she likes; the family, too, is free from worry about whether their religious observances will offend a nanny of a different faith.

Male Nannies, Anyone?

You may have noticed that so far in this book whenever there has appeared a pronoun standing in for a nanny, it has been "she." That is because in the real world today all but a small fraction of full-time childcare providers are female. Still, there *are* some male nannies out there, and the question may come up if one of them calls seeking to be interviewed for the job: Should you or shouldn't you?

Before I take on that issue, let me first take care of the first question that you may be wondering about: Is it legal to refuse to consider a nanny based solely on his sex?

The short answer, for most families, is yes. Working for a family is not like working for a large corporation. All kinds of personal considerations that have no place in the working environment of a factory or an office may reasonably figure into your home employment choice. The childcare provider is a member of your household, and is expected to provide services of an intimate nature: dressing small children, bathing them, helping them use the toilet. If you have a daughter, you are certainly within your rights, both as a parent and an employer, to preserve her sense of modesty and allow only a person of the same sex to provide the care required.

If you have sons, the issue becomes a little more complicated. You may be uncomfortable at the idea of a young man, bursting with hormonal energy, having intimate daily contact with your prepubescent boys. National crime statistics bear out the greater risk for sexual abuse of children by males, compared to females. But wouldn't it be discriminatory to prejudge any individual male applicant on the basis of broad population statistics?

I don't believe you have to. If you, the employer, are female, and you will be hiring a person for domestic duties in your own home, you simply need to define the job in such a way as to include some personal services for yourself as well as your children. Let us say that you will from time to time require assistance with your own wardrobe. You may need the person to arrive at an hour when you are likely to be in the shower, or at least not fully presentable to the opposite sex. Under such circumstances, it is reasonable and legal for an employer to consider the sex of a domestic employee relevant to the duties to be performed.

There are, however, certain circumstances under which you might not only want to consider a male applicant but might actively prefer to hire one. Many parents of boys see an advantage in having a carefully screened and experienced young man providing a positive male image in the home. Single mothers of boys (and sometimes girls, as well— especially if they are old enough to dress and bathe themselves without help) may especially seek out a male nanny to fulfill many of the functions society normally assigns to the father in the typical two-parent family. When the employer follows through with careful reference checking, and has received assurance from the male sitter's previous employers as to his proper and responsible behavior, then the employer should be able to place full confidence in a male nanny, expecting no less (and no more) of him than one would of a female in the same role.

On the Delicate Topic of National Stereotypes

Comedian Rita Rudner does a hilarious routine about selecting a nanny. Her husband, she confides, is wishing for one of those blond, free-spirited Scandinavian girls—while she has in mind "a matronly woman from one of the Baltic states."

It's funny, because it's true—we all tend to get these stereotypes in our head. But it's also a little dangerous. Surely one of the factors that led the Eappens to hire and then keep on young Louise Wood-ward, despite all misgivings they eventually developed concerning her work, was the simple fact of her Englishness. She *sounded* to most Americans like Mary Poppins. Proper. Sweet-natured. She was rosy-cheeked and neatly coiffed. But she was far from a Mary Poppins in reality, and by the time the parents realized it, it was too late to do anything about it.

It's worthwhile for parents who have not yet met any candidates to examine their own prejudices before they start hearing from foreign nationals over the phone. Each candidate deserves to be judged strictly on the basis of the record she presents and the competence she conveys. You not only need to guard against whatever discriminatory impulses you might harbor against an applicant from a particular foreign country, but you must also put aside consideration of anything unrelated to childcare skills that might tend to prejudice you *in her favor,* such as a charming Irish brogue, or a beautiful Indian sari, or the ability to dance the *hora.*

There are families, on the other hand, who have a particular need for a nanny of a certain ethnic heritage or linguistic background. Chinese-Americans, for example, might want to be sure their children get plenty of chances to practice their Mandarin, and so will hire only a nanny who is fluent in that language as well as English. Children being raised in a strict Muslim home, to take another example, could receive the most appropriate care from a nanny whose own religious roots give her knowledge of the required five daily prayers and the proper way to perform them. Such considerations may steer you toward a particular pool of applicants, but then out of that pool you will interview and choose strictly on each individual candidate's merits.

So you can see that the nationality issue is in some ways similar to the gender issue. Employers are permitted far more leeway in judging applicants than is usually the case in a typical business setting. To support parental choice about their children's upbringing, we must permit a certain degree of discrimination. Still, we owe it to ourselves and to the people we hire to judge each one fairly, focusing only on the individual's ability to perform the tasks required—including tasks specific to a family's cultural and personal way of life.

⏰ LINGUISTIC WARNING!

Never hire a nanny who cannot make herself easily understood in English. Even if you intend for your nanny to use her native language with your children on a daily basis, you should be satisfied that her English is good enough to be understood over the telephone in an emergency. Do not count on an ambulance dispatch service or a poison control center to have any translators on hand, even for a second language as common as Spanish. Your nanny's English proficiency should at least be good enough for her to follow the instructions on the back of any bottle of cleaning fluid concerning emergency treatment in case of ingestion. If you have any doubts about an applicant's language abilities in an emergency, give her a test of fluency before you hire.

✳ CHAPTER TWO ✳

USING AN AGENCY

The Allure of the Agency

*T*he back pages of parenting magazines are full of advertisements for nanny agencies, au pair agencies, and other childcare-related services. Here are a few examples of what advertisements promise:

"The ultimate in childcare placement. Excellent live-in and live-out nannies. Available immediately."

"Fully screened. Experienced. Full/Part Time. Live-in/Live-out. CPR-Trained."

"Carefully screened and personally interviewed."

"Background investigations."

"The best nannies . . . The best families . . . Simply the Best!! Since 1985."

"For peace of mind . . ." followed by the agency name.

How reassuring these words sound. How comforting to know that someone else, a trained professional nanny recruiter with decades of experience, will do your screening for you, putting forth only the very top candidates for you to interview. It's sounds like just the thing for any busy, two-career family. No time spent agonizing over the exact wording of ads, no running around to bulletin boards, no worrying about criminal records or suspended driving licenses.

Of course, you know such services do not come cheap. But if you'll be spending thousands of dollars a year on your nanny's salary and benefits, it doesn't seem so out of line to shell out a thousand or two more, to insure that you're getting the best.

Virtually every parent I interviewed who had used a nanny agency cited this as their main reason. But when I asked if they felt they'd gotten their money's worth, the number who answered "yes" fell far short of the "virtually all" in my initial group. I found that parents who did not use an agency had about the same level of satisfaction as those who did. It would seem, therefore, that many people would do just as well to put in the time it takes to mount a careful search, and save themselves some money.

I found that those who were happiest with their agencies tended to fall into four distinct types:

1. The very busy—those who had no time to spare in the search.

2. The very nervous—those who didn't fully trust their own ability to screen out bad nannies.

3. The very rich—those who considered the four-figure agency fee a minor expense, and who generally expected to pay extra for extra convenience.

4. Those with special requirements. These were parents of a child with a disability or parents looking for a nanny from a particular country or cultural background. The parents looked for and found an agency that specialized in finding nannies that fit the particular family's needs.

If you do not fall into any of these four categories, you might want to take a look at Chapter Three now. Read over what's involved in hiring independently, and if you feel you can handle the job, proceed. If you have any doubts, return to this chapter to find out how to select and work with the best agency in your area.

Selecting an Agency

Just as there are good nannies and bad nannies and all gradations in between, so it goes for nanny agencies.

It is not hard to find nanny agencies in most big cities and suburbs (and that covers about eighty percent of the U.S. population). Agencies know how to attract parents' attention. They buy ads in your local or regional parenting publications, including resource books and magazines. You will probably find ads in the Sunday magazine or "Lifestyle" supplement of your nearest big-city newspaper. If your area lacks specialized parenting publications, then just try the Yellow Pages, under "Childcare" or "Nanny." In any or all of these places you will see wonderfully designed ads, full of pictures of smiling young women cradling infants or playing with toddlers, all of whom look like the kind of nanny you would hire in a heartbeat.

But ads can't help you determine which is the best nanny agency. They can only tell you which one has the best marketing strategy. The thing to do is to find out from others who have had experience with a particular nanny agency how things really turned out. If possible, get the word of mouth about an agency's performance from a friend. Never rely exclusively on the telephone references supplied by the agency. Naturally the agency will only provide you with the names of its most satisfied customers. It's the parents who had some difficulties who will be able to give you the truest sense of the agency's ability to meet your childcare needs.

If you don't have any friends with agency hiring experience, then you'll need to call a few agencies yourself to get a sense of how they do business. To decide which agency to call first, read the ads and rule out any that do not supply the type of nanny you need. For example, an ad that carries the slogan "The very best in live-in childcare" should alert you to the fact that the agency does not place live-out help. If you are not offering a live-in situation, you have just saved yourself a phone call. Unless the ad includes the phrase, "full-time and part-time," it's a good bet the agency places only full-time workers. If you expect the nanny to do some housework, stay away from the agency whose ads say that it provides "professional quality childcare" and nothing more. Most high-end nannies expect the employer to have a separate housecleaner for all but the children's rooms.

The agency's ad may also give you a vague sense of the salary range by means of carefully chosen code words. For example, agencies that say they offer "affordable" child care mean they have moderate- to low-paid nannies. Agencies that use words or phrases like "exclusive" or "only the best" or go by snob-appeal names like "Carriage Trade Nannies," "Prestige Nannies," or "Elite Nannies" are generally trying to clue you in to the fact that their nannies earn top dollar. Start with those ads that seem targeted toward your income group and the housing arrangement and hours that suit you. Finally, check for geographic closeness—because you don't want to have to travel an hour and a half to see the agency's offices and fill out their forms. This should narrow your search down considerably, perhaps to two or three agencies.

Next, you need to get answers to some very specific questions. For each agency you check out, expect to spend about ten to twenty minutes on the telephone finding out the following:

1. **The fee.** How much is it, how is it to be paid (check or credit card?), and when and in what installments is it due? How much upon application, how much upon hiring? Is there a pre-application fee as well as the fee upon hiring, and if so, how much?

2. **Type of nanny.** Ask the agency representative to describe their typical nanny. Is she live-in or live-out? Full or part time? What level of education and experience?

3. **Cost.** What is the salary range the agency expects most of their nannies to earn? Ask the agency representative to give an example of top pay, average pay, and the minimum level of pay they might expect for one of their nannies for a forty-five-hour week.

4. **Special skills.** Mention driving; cooking; CPR certification; first-aid training; ability to work with certain disabilities or medical conditions such as juvenile diabetes, asthma, or Attention Deficit Disorder (ADD)—whatever is relevant to your situation.

5. **Availability.** Find out whether the agency has job-seekers right away, and if they are local or must be brought in by the employer from another part of the United States or abroad.

6. **Investigative services.** Exactly how much screening does the agency do? What sort of background checks: driving record? criminal record? credit history? in how many states? How many references are checked, and is the hiring family put in touch with those references for a personal chat?

7. **Guidance.** What role does the agency play in setting up interviews, and then helping you to evaluate and select the best candidate for your household?

8. **Follow-up.** This may be the single most important point. What does the agency do if you hire one of their candidates and it doesn't work out? Make your questions specific, to find out what would happen in a variety of everyday scenarios, such as: What if I hire one of your nannies and fire her after two weeks? After one month? After two? Three? Does the firing have to be for cause, and if so, how is cause established? How many replacement candidates will I be allowed to screen? What if I don't hire any of them? Ask about refund policies for all the above scenarios. Ask what happens if a client never does find a nanny from the agency's list.

WARNING: MONEY AT RISK!

Find out all you can about the agency's replacement/refund policies *before* you pay any money to that agency. If you do not like their refund/replacement policy, call another agency. You may discover that all the agencies you contact have much the same policy on refund and replacement. If that turns out to be the case, consider whether you would be willing to risk losing the fee in order to preserve your option to hire a good candidate from outside the agency. If the answer is no, then the agency approach is not for you. In that case, go straight to Chapter Three to learn about hiring without an agency (and without the agency fee)!

You may not find it so easy to get straightforward answers to these questions in a single phone call. Many agency representatives will be coy with you, trying to give you the impression that the subject is too complicated to be covered over the phone. They'll immediately start pressuring you to come in and talk—knowing that their best chance to sign you up as a client is to get you seated comfortably in their offices, where you can immediately be shown some tempting resumés and friendly-looking applicants' photos. Once you have some faces in front of you, it will become very difficult for you to resist the idea of getting started by filling out the employment questionnaire.

But resist you should, until you have had the chance to check out at least one or two competitors, other agencies that from their ads sound as if they're geared toward meeting the need for the type of nanny you want to hire. Of those you contact by phone, consider which was the most forthcoming with information, the most pleasant to deal with, the one you felt was most likely to be able to serve your needs. Call that agency back and make an appointment to go in.

Beware the agency that says they will send a representative to your home or office. It may sound like a timesaver, but it's also a way that a fly-by-night operation can appear to be more legitimate. You need to see that the agency has a proper office and that the office appears well staffed and organized. Many a parent has been scammed by an "agency" that has nothing more than an eye-catching ad, a nice voice over the telephone, and a P.O. box to receive their checks.

To avoid any doubts you may have about the business record of the agency before you visit it, you may want to check with your Better Business Bureau or local Chamber of Commerce, to find out how many complaints are on file about the agency, and how they were resolved.

At your first sit-down meeting in the agency's office you should find out:

- how long they've been in business
- how they got into the business
- how they do their recruiting of nannies
- where most of their nannies come from
- whether they offer (or require their nannies to take) any childcare, first aid, or safety courses
- what their philosophy is about the nanny-parent relationships

- how they see their role in mediating disputes that may crop up between the nanny and the employer

Expect at your first meeting that the agency representatives will be screening you, just as much as you are screening them. Part of an agency's proper role is to protect their nannies, to be sure that these women are not being placed in any dangerous or overly difficult situations. An agency will be able to attract a higher quality of nanny when they develop the reputation of dealing only with reputable people, the kind who would not exploit or abuse their employees.

If the meeting is going well and you are feeling confident that the agency does their business honestly and efficiently, then go ahead and get the paperwork started. You will probably be asked to submit an advance payment (with the balance due, typically, upon hiring) before you fill out their questionnaire. You will also be asked to sign a contract.

Very likely, if you are not a lawyer, you will not understand all of the provisions of the contract. That doesn't necessarily mean you must add to your costs the price of having a lawyer go over the contract. A simpler, cheaper way to handle this problem is for you to insist that they write down in plain English the meaning of the sentence or phrase you don't understand, right next to the legalese in the document, and all of the parties initial that language.

If they will not work with you to make the contract readable, using terms you understand and find fair, do not sign it. Do not work with that agency. Go back a few steps and take a second look at one of the other agencies you checked out—or, if you find that you are dissatisfied with the way that all of the agencies do business, skip the rest of this chapter and proceed directly to the chapter on hiring independently.

The Agency Questionnaire

Nearly all agencies use questionnaires to try to match employers with suitable nannies. A good agency questionnaire will be very detailed, perhaps four to six pages long. You will be asked to describe exactly what you are looking for in a nanny: what hours and what

READ THIS BEFORE YOU SIGN THAT CONTRACT!

Regardless of what oral assurances you are given, it is the agency's written contract that governs what will actually transpire. Take notes on all promises that agency representatives may make, and when it comes time to sign the contract, check your notes against what the contract says. If there is any assurance you have received orally that is not present in the contract, ask to have that assurance put down in writing, to be initialed by all parties. If the agency representative tells you that's not necessary, because "there's never been a problem on that issue before" or other words to that effect, don't be misled.

⏰ Be aware that you are only getting what the contract provides. If you don't see it in writing, it does not exist!

list of requirements. You will be asked to describe your children, their schedules, and the nanny's duties with each child.

It's good to have given some thought to these matters before you get to the agency.

Two very important rules, that will save you time and hassle if observed:

- Be scrupulously honest with the agency about the job you want done.
- Be realistic about your expectations of a nanny.

The first rule means that you will tell the agency straight out about anything difficult about your children or your working conditions. If your baby doesn't adjust well to strangers, say so. If he's a non-napper, up and running for the whole ten-hour workday, say so. If she has frequent tantrums, better to get it out now than to have the person quit on you in the middle of the first week. Tell the truth about yourself as well: If you often get home late and aren't always able to give the nanny advance word that extra time will be needed, say so. When it comes to the running of your household, spell out all the rules you intend to impose. If you don't allow the nanny or the kids to watch TV during certain hours, by all means, write those restrictions into the job description that you give to the agency.

Your frankness up front may well reduce the pool of applicants who would consider working for you—it's true—but you will also save yourself time you might have otherwise spent interviewing someone who would probably not last very long on the job. This frankness does not mean that you should make your children seem like terrors or your home seem like a sweatshop. By all means, point out everything wonderful about your kids, your house, your neighborhood, and the job routine. Just don't exaggerate, and definitely don't cover anything up.

One of nannies' biggest complaints about the parents they work for is that parents don't tell the whole truth upon hiring. (See Judy's Story, in the box on page 49.)

Although I believe you need to be honest in filling out the questionnaire, I also believe you need to be aware that in employment applications, others are seldom as honest in return. In fact, many, or perhaps most, people think it's to their advantage to fudge the truth here and there. In other words, be prepared to take the agency's descriptions of the nannies they represent with a grain of salt. You are warned right now that virtually every candidate you hear about is going to be called "a jewel" or a "wonderful girl." They will, of course, all be described with adjectives like "responsible," and "dependable" and "loving." You may even hear that ultimate accolade: "She is Mary Poppins, come to life."

Just remember, it's the agency's job to "sell" the applicants they have agreed to represent—and the real money for them is in turnover, placing each nanny relatively quickly, so that they can move on to the next case. From the minute they've got someone in their files, the push is on to get her hired. Don't pay too much attention to their claims about careful matching, or computer analysis of their clients' needs, because all the agencies make similar claims. Of course, they have an interest in your satisfaction, given that much of the agency's business comes from word of mouth—and your opinion will be important to them. But getting you matched up quickly is part of the bottom line,

TRUTH IN HIRING (JUDY'S STORY)

Yes, I would still have taken the job if I'd known about the older child's medication schedule. The thing is, I would have been better prepared, and I would have had more trust for the parents if they had only let me know in advance. As it was, my first day, they left for work and they said as they went out the door, "Oh, by the way, make sure he has his pill the minute he gets home from school. If he doesn't, he can become very aggressive." From the first, I felt it was going to be hard to build a bond with their son because I was always wondering what else they were hiding from me. The situation started out full of confusion and awkwardness, and really never got any better. I worked for them only three and a half months before I found my present family, where I'm very happy.

and to that end it will often make business sense to describe a mediocre girl as if she is the answer to a mother's prayers.

All you need to do is be aware that such puffery is common practice. And when you hear those seductive phrases, just keep saying to yourself, "Mary Poppins is a fictional character." With this truth firmly in mind, you will be less likely to be disappointed with the actual, less-than-magical applicants who show up at your door.

Setting Up the Interview

Soon after you've paid the initial fee and completed your questionnaire, the agency should begin offering you candidates. It's helpful, although not essential, to have access to a fax machine, so that the agency can send you written material about the nanny that will arrive the same day you hear about the candidate over the phone. Since, as mentioned above, agencies tend to oversell their clients on most applicants, anything you can get in writing from the candidate herself might help keep your expectations at a realistic level. Material you might be sent could include a résumé, a statement of career goals, or a short essay about her thoughts on certain childcare questions. Reading the nanny's ideas about nannying in her own writing can be very revealing. Agencies may fax photos, too.

What happens next depends somewhat on the way the agency operates or on your own preferences. Some agencies will set up the interview(s) for you. More commonly, you take the phone number of the top candidate(s) and call directly to set up interview(s). (If the nanny is not local, see the section on page 51 in this chapter about hiring from outside your area.)

There are those who advise calling the nanny's references before doing the interview. Since I strongly recommend a follow-up interview if you think you might hire the nanny, I advise checking the references between the first and second interviews.

Your first telephone contact with the nanny candidate is very important. You can save yourself an hour or more of interview time if you will just take five or ten minutes to chat with her over the phone. You should be doing more in this phone call than just setting up a convenient time for her to be interviewed in your home. You should be getting a sense of the way she conducts business.

Did she answer the telephone intelligibly? Politely?

Is her voice clear and pleasant, her use of language grammatical?

Does she seem interested in the interview? Did she sound curious about the job? Did she ask any questions about you, your situation, your children?

Although the agency has already provided you with some basic information about her background and work experience, it's important to have her tell you herself, in your first phone call, the same facts about herself that she gave the agency. If she has fictionalized any part of her résumé, discrepancies may become apparent as she talks off the top of her head. Do be sure to check what she tells you against the written history that she has provided to the agency.

Assuming the candidate sounds good over the phone, go ahead and schedule the interview. This should be in your own house, not your office, and certainly not in the nanny agency's office. You need to show the candidate around her potential working environment. You also need to see whether she is able to get to your house on time for

> ⏰ Do not proceed any further with a candidate whose agency résumé is at odds with her own description of herself over the phone.

the appointment. You will want to find out how she interacts with your child(ren).

If the nanny sounds less than suitable over the phone, tell her you are not ready to set up interviews just yet, but are waiting until you have spoken to a few more applicants, and will start setting up interviews later on. Then call the agency back, and tell the representative what it was about the nanny you found disquieting. Maybe she answered your questions in monosyllables, maybe her accent was too thick for you to understand, maybe she just sounded bored or flippant or she came right out and said something that clashed with your views on sound childrearing practices (for example, she wanted to know exactly what times a day your baby was to be given a bottle, when you believe in feeding on demand). Being specific with the agency will give them an idea of how to match you with a better choice on the next go-round.

Assuming your phone contact went well, then skip ahead to Chapter Four, Interviewing and Reference Checking.

The Out-of-Area Hire

I would like to make this section short and to the point. *Don't do it!* End of section.

However, so many parents bring in nannies from other parts of the world (and many times, I have to admit, they end up satisfied with their choice) that I know I must provide some arguments for my strong stand against this option.

The main reason I advise against out-of-area hiring is the lack of opportunity for an in-person interview. If you read all the sections in Chapter Four about interviewing, you will see the importance I place on conducting a four-stage interview, which will maximize your chances of spotting trouble at each step of the process. With an out-of-area hire, on the other hand, you are usually limited to a telephone interview or two. You simply cannot get a good enough sense of what the nanny will be like with your children, unless you get the chance to observe her in real life.

What makes the situation even more dicey is that out-of-area hires are nearly always brought over as live-ins. They are typically able to relocate only with the promise of a place to stay, which means an added complication for you if, for whatever reason, you decide to let her go. You not only have to find a replacement nanny, but you have to do so while your home is still being occupied with the one you no longer want. If she has come to your home from far away, her travel back may be expensive and difficult to arrange—and she may even refuse to leave.

Given these obvious and serious risks, why then do so many parents still use agencies that link them up with nannies from other areas? The answer is: the very real nanny shortage that prevails in many of our big cities and suburbs. When you advertise for a nanny on your own, you may be shocked to find not a single applicant who meets the very reasonable standards you expect from a childcare professional. Meanwhile, you see ads for nanny agencies in newspapers and magazines leading you to believe that there are plenty of qualified nannies available, but just not in your immediate area, and that the agencies know where they are. Ads promise that through an agency you will be put in touch with dozens of bright, ambitious, hard-working girls who would be only too happy to come to your home and take care of your children.

It's easy to start forming an image in your mind about the sort of nanny an agency will be able to produce. You're thinking about a broad-faced Wisconsin farm girl, or a Wyoming rancher's daughter, and you daydream that maybe right now she is busy fixing a three-course pancake breakfast for her triplet baby brothers. You can almost smell the bacon!

When you find yourself conjuring up a vision of wholesome folksiness, it's good to remember that old bit of farm wisdom: Never buy a pig in a poke—especially when you could get a chance to see for yourself. In other words, as long as there are qualified nannies who live in your own area that you could get to interview in person, try to hire one of them. Given a choice between an agency that recruits locally and one that brings in nannies from elsewhere, go with the agency that has local nannies.

This is by no means a hard and fast rule. Some exceptions are:

- Your family is from a different culture and strongly desires a nanny who shares your own background and childrearing cus-

---

"THE AGENCY SENT ME CINDI . . . AND ONLY CINDI"
(IRENE'S STORY)

After her first, wonderful long-term nanny told her she would be moving out of state, Irene decided to use a nanny agency to find a replacement. The one she chose ran appealing ads showing pictures of friendly looking faces of girls mainly from the Midwest and Rocky Mountain states. Within a few days Irene was put in touch with Cindi, who lived in a small town in Idaho. The agency director assured Irene that Cindi would be a great nanny, but also led her to believe that there would be no problem getting a replacement if things did not work out.

Right from the start Irene lodged her complaints against Cindi with the agency. Cindi, at age eighteen, acted like a girl five years younger; she was homesick; she was afraid to go out in the big city on her own; she appeared overwhelmed from day one by the tasks involved in caring for Irene's toddler boy and baby girl. The agency director kept telling Irene to be patient and give the girl time to adjust. She promised to send other candidates to be interviewed if Irene was still dissatisfied a few weeks later. Irene persisted in complaining, but was often put off over the phone, or had her calls go unreturned. Then, by the time she finally got through to the agency head, she was informed that the trial period had ended, and there would be no replacements, and no refunds of any amount!

Irene now has a lawsuit pending against the agency.

toms. For example, you come from India, your family speaks Hindi at home, and you want your children to be immersed in the religion and customs of your mother country. You learn of an agency with a U.S. office that recruits well-trained candidates from India who have green cards, or who are about to receive green cards permitting them to work in the United States. (If you fit this picture and are tempted to go with an agency that recruits overseas, be especially wary of one that would leave it up to you or the nanny to handle immigration matters. You will doubtless end up with an illegal immigrant, with all the attendant risks of deportation for her and fines for you, not to mention the disruption of the child-nanny emotional bond.)

or:

- The nanny has already worked for your friend or relative in her place of origin and so comes with a personal reference who can serve as a stand-in for your in-person evaluation.

If neither of the above scenarios describe your situation, then I would urge you to consider an out-of-area hire only if you or the nanny can manage to meet for at least one long face-to-face interview in advance of hiring. If, for example, you travel for business or family reasons to the state or country where the nanny now resides, arrange to conduct a lengthy and thorough interview in her home.

If, after all these cautions, you still feel an agency that recruits out-of-area nannies can provide what you're looking for, proceed with due caution:

- Get assurances in writing that the agency will arrange for an alternate place for the nanny to stay should you decide, within a reasonable period of time (which must be spelled out in your contract), that you do not want to keep her on.
- If the contract holds you responsible for her airfare to the place of employment, make sure you will be refunded some or all of the cost if she leaves the job within a specified period of time. Make sure the amount and time limit is specified in the contract.
- For an out-of-the-country hire, you may want to have an immigration lawyer advise you on the legality of the nanny's work

"DEIRDRE SOUNDED GREAT OVER THE TELEPHONE, BUT . . ." (MARGARET'S STORY)

My husband found this wonderful website on the Internet run by an Irish nanny agency. You could click on a nanny's name and see her résumé and sometimes a photo, too. It looked like they had dozens of wonderful girls available, when in our city we'd had a hard time finding anyone even worth our time to interview. We contacted the agency, and it all sounded pretty easy. We selected a few names, were given telephone numbers, and started making calls. The third girl we talked to over the telephone sounded best. Her name was Deirdre and she'd been a nanny in the Boston area before. We interviewed her for maybe ten or fifteen minutes over the phone, and then we called the family she'd worked for, and they said they'd been quite happy with her. Since everything sounded good, we went ahead and sent her a plane ticket. Within hours of her arrival we realized our mistake. I'm sure we would never have hired her if we'd interviewed her in person. She wasn't at all the way she sounded over the phone. We expected someone neat and quiet and something of a homebody. Deirdre turned out to be sloppy beyond belief, raucous and wild about her favorite rock bands, and not all that interested in our two-year-old son's activities. She used to take his favorite stuffed animal, a mouse, and hold it up by the tail and joke that it looked like a rat, and she'd pretend to call a rat-catcher to get rid of it. He couldn't understand that she was joking, and of course he'd start to cry. We asked her not to say those things to him, and the second time she did it anyway, we fired her. But then getting her out of the house was another story. And not a pretty one. We also tried to sue the agency to get back our $1,400 fee . . . but we ended up with nothing, because it was too complicated to litigate against an overseas business.

papers and inform you of any risk you may be assuming if proper documentation cannot be obtained.

- Once the out-of-area hire arrives, resist pressure from the agency, from the nanny herself, or from within your own family to overlook any problems that may develop. Since undoing an out-of-area hire can be complicated, you may find yourself saying, "Oh, we can work out this or that problem." With a local nanny you wouldn't have to—you could make a change, which is, quite often, the safest course. Do not allow your thinking about trust and safety to be influenced by the distance or the expense involved in undoing the deal.

※ CHAPTER THREE ※

HIRING INDEPENDENTLY

The Downside of Agencies

*F*or parents whose primary concern is safety, the question is: Which hiring method offers us the greatest flexibility over hiring and firing decisions—the agency approach or the do-it-yourself approach? After dozens of interviews with parents who had hired one way or the other (and quite a few who had tried both), I find the evidence pointing strongly to one conclusion: Independent hiring is the *safest* way to acquire a nanny.

Why? Because giving an outside party, the agency, a strong financial interest in your hiring decision puts too much pressure on you to accept one of its choices, and to act within the time limits imposed by the agency's contract. It also puts too much pressure on you (out of fear that you will get little or nothing for your fee) to keep on a nanny about whom you may have doubts.

What about the argument that agencies are great time-savers for busy parents? Since the safety-oriented parents that I interviewed felt obliged to double-check the nanny's references themselves, little time was saved.

As for the criminal record checking, driving record checking, and other background checks performed by an agency, I have found that parents can also accomplish such investigations on their own, as well or better than some agencies. Parents can purchase the services of a specialized private investigator, one who focuses exclusively on nanny-checking, or they can use a general investigations agency, and receive the requested information for a fraction of a nanny agency's fee.

You may think that a reputable nanny agency will give you access to a wider pool of good nannies. In some cities there is without a doubt a serious labor shortage for qualified childcare workers, and so in those cases there could well be some truth to this assertion; still, with a little persistence and creativity on your part, as well as some helpful hints from this chapter, you should be able to place yourself in the best possible position to attract the attention of your area's top job-hunting nannies.

This chapter will show you how to:

- target your "nanny wanted" notice to places where the good nannies are most likely to be found
- screen out undesirable applicants quickly and with a minimum of hassle
- find soon-to-be available nannies *before* a nanny agency spots them and recruits them into its fee-based pool of applicants

By hiring independently you will accomplish three very important objectives:

1. You will save yourself the $1,000 to $2,000 fee a typical agency will charge for its services.
2. You will retain control over the hiring process, so that you don't get locked into a particular pool of candidates being put forward by a particular agency.
3. (I saved the most important for last.) You will be able to fire without hesitation, should you conclude that your first choice is wrong for the job.

Most agencies will not refund any money if you fire after the initial limited probationary period has ended. (This could be anywhere from two weeks to two months.) Even if you fire within the probationary period, you will still be under financial pressure to accept a substitute from the same agency within a limited period of time—or again risk losing the fee. Having to worry about fees distracts you from the far more important issue, which is the safety and well-being of your children.

Running Your Own Search—It Doesn't Have to Be Intimidating

The key is to leave yourself enough time. With enough forethought to plan each move carefully, you can do the job right; you can be as thorough about checking out credentials as any agency professional; and you can have confidence that nothing important has been glossed over, because you have personally overseen all phases of the process. You are never left to blindly trust the judgment of some financially motivated group of strangers.

You need to proceed one step at a time according to a logical plan. By taking on each task in sequence, not moving on until you have completed the previous step to your satisfaction, you will not become intimidated or overwhelmed by the responsibilities involved.

The steps are:

1. Decide what you're looking for.

2. Think of the widest variety of places where you might be likely to find what you're looking for.

3. Compose a separate notice or advertisement tailored to each of those places where you think good nannies can be found.

4. Prescreen by telephone all those responding to your notices or advertisements.

5. Set up interviews according to the four-step process described in Chapter Four.

6. Check references as described in Chapter Four.

7. For those jobs involving driving, have your top applicant complete a test-drive as described in Chapter Four.

8. Have a background check completed on your top applicant (court records and driving record check) by a specialized nanny-checking agency or a private investigator. (This step may not be necessary if the nanny's previous employer has already had such a check performed and can vouch for the results.)

9. Negotiate to hire as described in Chapter Five.

At first glance this may seem like a long list. But consider this: You'd have to do steps 5, 6, 7, and 9 for an agency-hired nanny, as well. The rest of this chapter will be devoted to walking you through steps 1, 2, 3, 4, and 8.

Step One: Decide What You're Looking For

Pretend you are working with an agency and are filling out a questionnaire that has you state what you're looking for in writing. Here are some of the questions you should be able to answer before you start the search (key issues are in **boldface**):

Will the nanny **live-in or live-out?**

How many **hours per week?**

How are the hours to be structured (**weekly schedule**)?

Anticipated need for **overtime**: About how many times a month will you need the nanny to come in earlier than usual or stay later?

What **salary** range? You don't need to be specific—just have a general sense of whether your weekly salary falls within the high, medium, or low range for your region.

What **benefits** are in your package? Are you offering health insurance? Payment of employment taxes (hers as well as yours)? Paid vacation time? All federal holidays?

What **term of employment** are you offering (that is, how many years do you anticipate keeping a nanny)? How long do you want this hire to commit to working for you, if all goes well?

If she is an immigrant to the United States, will you require proof of her **work documents**? (See the box on page 62 for discussion of the legal-versus-illegal problem.)

Will **travel** with the family be required for the job?

Is **driving** required? If so, must she have her own car?

Are there any **non-childcare duties** (such as light housekeeping)? By the time you do interviews you should be prepared to answer specific questions about any extra duties and what proportion of the nanny's day is to be spent attending to them.

Is **swimming** a required skill? Do you want Red Cross Lifesaving Certification.

Is a certain **educational level** required? For example, will you require that the nanny already be CPR certified, or would you allow her to take classes later for CPR certification? What about first-aid training, childcare courses, or a high school degree?

Must she be a **nonsmoker**? (See Chapter Four, page 85, for a discussion of why even parents who smoke should not permit their nanny to do so.)

Is there a **minimum age**? Some parents, for example, when hiring a full-time caretaker for a child under age two will set a minimum age of twenty-one as a job requirement.

Do you only want someone with a certain minimum **level of experience**? You may wish to limit your interviews to those candidates who have worked at least three years as a nanny or in some other childcare capacity. Parents of infants may wish to interview only those candidates with experience working with babies under a year old.

Any requirement for **physical qualities** (such as high energy level, ability to run or climb after children on a playground)?

What are the main **emotional qualities** you are seeking? Stability? Cheerful disposition? Maturity?

What **work habits** are most important to you? Punctuality? Loyalty? Enthusiasm for the task at hand? Creativity?

Which **personality type** do you consider most desirable? Outgoing and bubbly versus quiet and low-key? To answer that question you must take into account your own child's personality type—whether he or she is extroverted and quick to accept new people, or shy and easily frightened.

Are you looking for fluency in any **language other than English**? For example, do you need someone who can supervise homework assigned by the teacher of the child's after-school Japanese class?

Do you seek someone familiar with certain **cultural or religious practices**? Do you need someone who can keep a kosher kitchen, or

who can help the child put on his prayer shawl and other accoutre-
ments correctly?

Do you need someone who can work with a child who has **special
needs**? Must your nanny be able to work hand-in-hand with your
child's physical therapist, administer medication, or cope with certain
behavioral or emotional problems?

You need not list every detail you're hoping to find in your notices
or advertisements. The above list is mainly to help you conceptualize
the sort of nanny you will be hiring. It's not a wish list, because you

---

LEGAL VERSUS ILLEGAL

You probably know all the reasons you should insist on a legally
documented nanny.

- There are costly penalties if you are caught.
- Think of the disruption for you and your children if she's
  subject to deportation.
- Think of the pressure you'll be under to underwrite her
  legal battle to stay put. (Can you afford to help out? But
  think about how guilty you might feel if you didn't.)
- Think about the trouble you might stir up if it got out
  that you had violated a federal law. (Does the name Zoe
  Baird ring a bell?)

That's all on one side. On the other side is the very real possibility that the only satisfactory respondents to your ad will be
women who are in this country without proper work papers. What
to do?

I leave the decision to you, but keep in mind at all times the
best interests of your child. You may find it helpful to hear how
other parents have fared. See pages 63 and 64 for some interesting
responses to the interview question "Have you ever hired an illegal immigrant as a nanny? Were there any problems?"

recognize at the outset that no single person is going to embody every trait that you're looking for. Once you have identified the qualities and skills most important to you, you can begin to focus on where a person who fits the bill would likely be found.

SUE'S STORY

All of my nannies (five in the past thirteen years) have been here without working papers. I've had Rosa from El Salvador, Anya from Poland, Jill from England, Doreen from Ireland, and now I have Nina from Trinidad. None of them has ever had any trouble from the Immigration and Naturalization Service (INS). Rosa and Anya were eventually able to get green cards. Jill married an American and moved to another state. Doreen moved back to Ireland, and we've gone over to visit her twice. We still love her and consider her part of our family. Nina is here on a student visa, and she may actually go back to school next year, finish her degree, and then decide whether to try to get a green card or go home. Personally, I hope she stays. She is a wonderful nanny, far better than any of the legal ones who answered my ad. That's all I care about—who's best to look after my kids. Not what some bureaucrat tells me I should be doing.

Step Two: Think About Where to Find the Nanny You Want to Hire

The search for a good nanny becomes less daunting when you begin to realize how many excellent avenues there are for a nanny to learn about your job opening. One of these avenues will work for you. In this section we'll consider:

- **word of mouth** (also known as "the Nanny Network")
- **schools** (colleges, universities, nursing schools, nanny schools, nursery schools, and other educational institutions)

KATHLEEN'S STORY

My husband and I run our own business. Our accountant told us if we hired someone legal, we could deduct a certain percentage of the childcare costs from our taxes, and it's tempting. . . . Unfortunately, we haven't yet met anyone who is both qualified and legal. Where we live, good nannies are very hard to find. When we heard that our neighbor's nanny, Laila—she's from Somalia—was looking for a job, we snapped her up. Our children knew her and we already liked her a lot. Yes, we're aware of the risks. We know we can't take her with us when we visit my husband's folks in Montreal, because of the ID checks at the border. It makes me mad, because I think our immigration laws are made mostly by men who don't know what it's like these days for working moms. Laila is not only a great nanny, but she's exactly the sort of hard-working person this country ought to encourage to become a citizen. Well, that's my speech for today.

- **bulletin boards** found at gathering spots for kids and their caregivers (including community centers, churches and temples, swimming or tennis clubs, libraries, co-op markets, kids' consignment stores, kids' bookstores, skating rinks, ballet classes, pediatric offices, fast-food restaurants with indoor playspaces, peewee sports events, Gymboree or other parent-child exercise facilities—wherever small children are likely to be found in the company of a nanny)
- **classified ads** in community newspapers, local parenting magazines, ethnic newspapers, and other specialized publications that a nanny might be likely to read

You may have noticed that I do not include a bullet for large circulation daily newspapers. That's because I strongly believe the help-wanted pages of most big city papers will largely be a waste of your time. Sure, you'll get dozens of calls in response to your ad, but of that number perhaps only one or two will be worth an interview. The other avenues for nanny recruitment are much more effective than mass-circulation newspaper advertising, so my advice is to avoid spending the money on such an untargeted approach.

Word of Mouth

Far and away your best resource for learning about good, safe nannies will be other nannies, and the people who have employed them. When someone you know and respect, someone with a family much like your own, tells you she personally knows of a nanny she thinks is great, and that the nanny will be job hunting soon . . . bingo!

The key is to get yourself plugged into "the Nanny Network." You've got to do some legwork, and some telephone work, as well. First, call everyone you can think of who has ever employed a good nanny. Ask them to ask their own nannies if they know of anyone good who is looking for a job. Nannies tend to be up on who else is in the market for a job . . . and they will probably tell you candidly, too, if a certain soon-to-be-available nanny is one to avoid!

Of course, the luck of your timing plays a large role in how well the nanny network will work for you. You may well discover, after you've called your friends, your co-workers, your neighbors, (and don't forget your spouse's friends and co-workers), that nobody knows of anyone just yet who is good and happens to be about to change jobs. That's okay—just expand your circle of contacts. Bring the subject up every chance you get: Ask your friends to ask their friends; mention your search to people you've just met at parties; strike up conversations with the other people at your bus stop; go over and chat with other parents you see at your neighborhood playgrounds, shops, and school events. If you don't normally participate in a lot of neighborhood activities, start! You'll greatly increase your circle of contacts with people who either employ nannies or are currently nannies themselves. Even if you don't find someone to fill your position this time around, it's still of benefit for you to have these connections, so that when you do eventually find a good nanny, you'll be aware of a whole social scene for her to fit into, preventing the problem of social isolation from developing. (See Chapter Six for other suggestions to create a pleasant working environment for your nanny and your children.)

Not only are friends, neighbors, and other nannies a great source for information about available nannies, they're also a time-saver, because you get a reliable personal reference at the same time. Generally, word of mouth gets you a better nanny than you'll find from posted notices or newspaper ads, because the best nannies don't need to do a lot of job-hunting. They just get the word out on "the Nanny Network" that they're looking, and they tend to get snapped up by the fortunate set of parents who happen to be the first to catch the news.

Because the best nannies tend to be long-term committers, they come into the job market infrequently, so you will need to be patient. An employer intent on finding a nanny through personal contacts should allow two or three months extra for the search, and be flexible about when the job can begin, to fit in with the needs of a nanny's current employer. In some cases, if you know of someone good who will be needing a new position six months or even a year from now, you may wish to seek short-term help, in order to be free to hire the nanny you want.

Schools

Younger nannies (age thirty or under) tend to have wonderful plans for their future. Nannying is a good temporary career choice for the young woman who one day would like to go into pediatrics, nursing, teaching, child development, child psychology, or any other helping profession requiring an advanced degree. In order to accomplish her goal, a nanny would take classes in the evenings while working full-time during the day. Another common strategy is for the nanny to work full time for a few years, living-in to save on rent and other expenses, until she has enough money saved up for her tuition. When she has the needed amount, she quits her job to become a full-time student.

These nannies are reachable through the job placement centers of your local colleges, universities, and other educational institutions. Call the schools in your area and ask to be connected with their "career center" or "student employment service"—whatever the job placement office is called. Ask what you should do to enter your nanny opening into their system. The job placement counselor on the other end of the line will probably run down a list of questions from a form for you to answer: questions such as category of job (answer, "childcare"); hours; salary; duties; requirements; and so on. From your answers a notice will be composed and placed in a book or file that job-hunting students may flip through.

Some job placement offices ask that you mail or fax in a notice that you write yourself. In that case, turn to page 70 in this book for a discussion about how to make your job notice appealing to the best sort of nanny.

One caveat—while I have heard many wonderful stories about great student-nannies, I have also heard one fairly consistent complaint: Student-nannies follow the academic calendar. They may be gone after the next semester. They go off on required summer internships. They go home to their own parents' homes for the holidays. They can't come in during Exam Week.

If the commitment of a full-time nanny is what you need, and you find your applicant through a student job placement center, make sure that student understands that your need for childcare does not go away during Spring Break. If the student is able to juggle a part-time course load with full-time childcare, then she will probably do a good job for you. If she has misjudged her own time constraints, you may find yourself looking for a new nanny sooner than you had expected.

Colleges and universities are not the only educational institutions that may yield good nannies. Preschools and elementary schools have teachers and aides who occasionally will be interested in working for a family rather than an institution. Because preschool teachers are generally so poorly paid, a job as a full-time nanny may even be a step up on the economic ladder. Even if none of the employees of the school are interested in your notice, there's a good chance that another parent or nanny will see it and call to tell you about someone who may soon be available.

There are also nanny training schools that you may contact in your search. Not every state has one, so you will want to do some research to find out if there is one nearby. (The worldwide web is a good source of information; just type in "nanny school" and you should be able to pull up a current list of such institutions. The Resource Guide at the back of this book lists several websites that include links to lists of nanny schools.)

If you do not happen to live within driving distance of a nanny school, you may still want to contact the school about hiring one of its graduates from afar—keeping in mind all the cautions found on pages 51–56 about the hazards of hiring anyone sight unseen. Always find some way to arrange at least one face-to-face meeting before you commit to a nanny.

Bulletin Boards

Good nannies are active nannies. They just don't sit around the house all day with their charges, watching the soaps. They take them to playgrounds, to classes, to the pediatrician's office, to playgrounds, to stores, to the library, to church or temple, to children's classes, to the ice cream parlor, to sports events, to kid-friendly restaurants, to the neighborhood pool, to many other places. Just think of the places you take your own child: Which of those places has a bulletin board?

To compose your notice, read the section on that subject starting on page 70. Be sure to include in your notice a line, or at least a phrase, specially tailored to the bulletin board of each particular location you've chosen. For example, if you're posting your notice at the skating rink, you might vary your standard job description with the following details:

> . . . active, outgoing nanny needed to care for two little girls, ages 7 and 3, who love to skate in the winter and swim in the summer.

With appropriately targeted language you may catch the eye of a part-time skating instructor who is looking for steadier, full-time work, as well as any job-hunting nanny who chances to be at the rink. You will also be sending a message to any applicant who thinks of babysitting as literally *sitting* that you are looking for someone who isn't afraid to get onto the ice with kids; you won't accept a passive type.

Before you post your notice, make sure you know and follow all the rules for each particular bulletin board. Many have size restrictions, limiting you to a three-by-five-inch index card, or perhaps a half-size sheet of paper. Find out whether the notice must be dated, and if so, how many days after the posting date the notice will be removed. Does the date have to be in a particular corner?

Pay some attention to what your notice looks like. Hand-scrawled writing on a white piece of paper is just not very enticing, no matter what the content may be. Laser-printed copy, done in a clean, readable font, is the way to go. Be sure to put your phone number (including area code) in a prominent position. It's also helpful to specify calling times.

Try to include color and graphics on your posting, if you can. An appealing image will make your job seen more appealing, as well as make it stand out from the other competing notices for nannies. There are many software programs that allow you to select from a menu of images, sorted by category, to insert into your copy. See page 71 for an example of an ad created from a card- and flyer-making program

To insure that a nanny will get your number, even if she doesn't have a pen and paper on hand at the time, you may want to include tear-off tags, each with your phone number, along the bottom or side edge of your notice (see the sample on page 71).

Advertising in Newspapers and Magazines

Does your neighborhood, subdivision, or county have its own local paper? Does it come out at least twice a month? Does it have a classified section with at least two or three columns regularly devoted to childcare employment? Then you can bet that nannies in your area know about it and read it whenever they are thinking of switching jobs.

Your local area may also have a monthly magazine aimed at families. Check to see if it carries classifieds for childcare positions.

Don't forget to check out "positions wanted" ads which some families will submit for their nannies to help them transition to a new job.

A sometimes overlooked but fertile source of nannies is the local newspaper aimed at a particular ethnic group. If you live in the New York City area I especially recommend the *Irish Echo*. Its classifieds are chock full of ads from parents seeking nannies, and nannies seeking positions. Its popularity among nannies and families goes well beyond the Irish community; indeed, one family that placed an ad in that publication (and eventually found a great nanny through the ad) reported that nannies from many ethnic backgrounds responded, including Jamaicans, Dominicans, Haitians, Brazilians, non-ethnic Americans, and an Englishwoman—but none who were actually Irish.

Especially if you are looking for someone who can help bring your children up in the customs and rituals of your ethnic tradition, you would be well advised to advertise in a specialized ethnic paper. Big cities typically have weeklies or dailies published in many languages, among them: Chinese, Japanese, Vietnamese, Korean, Hindi and other Indian languages, Russian, Polish, and Tagalog (the language of the Philippines)—as well as the expected Spanish, French, and German. Just be aware of the caution on page 39 about the need for proficiency in English. You always want to be sure that your foreign-born nanny speaks English well enough to communicate effectively with rescue workers or ambulance dispatchers in an emergency.

Step Three: What Your Notice or Advertisement Should Say

Now that you know where to post your notice or fax in your ad, you need to decide what to say. The first principle is: *Longer is better.* If the cost per word is reasonable (and in most local circulation or specialized papers, that tends to be the case), then be sure to write in all those qualities and characteristics that are most important to you. By spelling out more of what you want in the ad, you will spend less time on the telephone weeding out people who don't meet your minimum requirements. Besides, if you're too brief, how will your potential nanny know how wonderful your children are, and how great a job opportunity you are offering?

Of course, you must check to be sure you have included all the basic facts: What location? Full-time or part-time? Live-in or live-out? How many children? What ages/gender? What general duties? Be sure to mention anything out of the ordinary, such as special care needed for a child with a disability. Give the phone number or numbers at which you wish to receive inquiries—and if it's an answering machine, say so. (Many nannies will just keep hanging up on a machine, preferring to keep trying to get the actual employer on the line.) It's a very

NANNY WANTED
Woodley Park Neighborhood

We're a friendly family with 2 girls, ages 6 and 3, looking for a reliable, energetic, outgoing nanny to work 40–45 hours a week. Excellent pay and benefits. Live-out, or apartment can be arranged if needed. Job requirements: nonsmoker, driver's license, references. Must take First Aid/CPR class if not already certified. Duties include: making kids' meals, reading to them, supervising activities, arranging outings.

Call 202–555–0000 (9 A.M–9 P.M)

NANNY NEEDED Spring Valley Area We're looking for an experienced, mature, responsible person to take care of our high-energy 3-year-old boy and 4-month-old girl. Must be legal, speak English, have good references, and drive. Excellent pay and benefits for someone who can provide safe, loving care, and who doesn't mind reading *Green Eggs and Ham* for the 100th time. Call between 9 A.M. and 5 P.M. and leave message on machine.	202-555-6767 202-555-6767 202-555-6767 202-555-6767 202-555-6767 202-555-6767 202-555-6767 202-555-6767

A Nanny Notice with side tear-off tags.

good idea to suggest limited times to call—that is, unless you really *like* to hear the phone ring at 6 A.M. or midnight.

A few pointers and tips:

Don't abbreviate too much. Don't write "N/smkr" for "Nonsmoker." Don't put "Lic. Drvr. Only" to indicate your need for a licensed driver. You want a nanny, not a CIA cryptographer.

Put your best selling points up front. Your best chance to attract a good nanny is to let her know your job has what all good nannies want:

> Top pay, excellent benefits for highly qualified person.

Can't afford to offer what nannies want most? Then sell by your personalities, how pleasant it will be to work for you:

> Delightful children, warm, friendly household.

Kids can be a handful? Then sell your job by offering some special benefit—flexible hours, perhaps, or a car for the nanny's exclusive use, or a private live-in suite. Think of whatever you have to offer that makes working for you an attractive deal, and better than working for some other family down the street. (If you have nothing extra to offer, you probably are not going to be able to attract that nanny who has a little something extra, either.)

Most other nanny ads fail in this regard. Most ads are simply a catalog of what the employer requires. They tell the nanny, "I want this or that from you," but give little sense that the employer is willing to give very much in return. *Always try to look at your own ad as if you yourself were job hunting.* If it doesn't sound appealing to you, it won't to a nanny either.

On the other hand, you don't want to oversell. You may think that your children are so adorable that it's really a treat to spend the day with them for six bucks an hour . . . but you can bet that no nanny thinks that way. Nannying is a tough job, and those who do it well are worthy of respect (though they all too seldom get it). Avoid making your ad sound cutesy or as if written by the baby:

> Won't you be my nanna? I'm nine months old and I'm looking for someone to give me lots of lov'n' care!

Ads like that don't convey a sense of dignity the nanny wants, nor does it help to establish the businesslike relationship you intend to build with the nanny.

The copy below provides a good example of an appealing newspaper ad.

> NANNY NEEDED. Full-time live-in to care for 9-month-old girl. Must drive, have good references, and be CPR certified or willing to take

course. Good pay, friendly household, separate live-in suite, opportunity to travel with family. Call Ms. Adler between 10 A.M. and 4 P.M.,
212–555–1234.

BEDTIME READING AS A JOB QUALIFICATION

Lots of ads say "fluent English required," but lots of nannies
who are minimally literate in English will answer those ads, thinking themselves qualified simply because they know enough English to answer the telephone, grocery shop, drive, and perform
all the basic household tasks.

If "basic" is all you're looking for in a nanny, then go ahead
and interview someone who can communicate at a functional
level. However, if you want your child to spend the day in the
company of an adult who can provide the sort of stimulation and
quality of care that you would provide yourself if you stayed home,
then indicate such desire in your ad. The fastest, most efficient
way to do that is to list "bedtime reading" as one of the job
qualifications.

When you interview, you will check to see that the nanny is
not faking it when she claims this skill. Question her about what
books she prefers for children of various ages. If she isn't familiar
enough with kids' books to name at least two or three favorites,
then she's not an experienced reader to children. But if she answers in a voice filled with enthusiasm, "I really love *Goodnight
Moon!*" and she starts to recite a few lines, you know you've got
a good one, so go for it!

Step Four: Prescreen Your Applicants

If there is one solid advantage to using an agency, it's the agency's
ability to prescreen the applicants for you. Any half-decent agency will

weed out the inexperienced, the illiterate, the unwashed, and other undesirables, so that you won't have to spend too much time on the phone politely turning away unqualified inquiries.

Still, if you know ahead of time what you are looking for, and you check each caller to be sure she meets those minimum requirements, you should be able to end a phone call from an obviously unqualified applicant within a minute or less.

What should you screen for?

Intelligibility. If you can't understand the applicant easily over the phone, you can bet that your child won't be able to either. And neither would a 911 operator responding to an emergency at your home.

Good telephone manners. You want to interview only the sort of person who knows how to behave in a social or business setting. If the person does not know how to make a job inquiry over the phone, you can be sure the person will also not know how to deal politely and effectively with your child's doctor, preschool teacher, your neighbors, or your boss who may call on the phone. (If you're thinking, that won't matter, because I'll simply instruct my nanny to let the answering machine pick up during the day, read the section in Chapter Seven explaining why, for safety's sake, the nanny should always answer your phone during the day.)

Basic qualifications. Even though you have listed your minimum requirements in your ad, you will be shocked to discover how many callers have either not read your ad carefully or have decided to ignore your stated qualifications. When your ad says "Must have own car," be prepared for calls from numerous nannies who don't even know how to drive. Ask for someone who can read books to your toddler and supervise your third-grader while he does his homework, and you will be sure to get at least one call from someone who hardly speaks English. The first order of business with each caller should be for her to confirm that she meets all the basic requirements you have listed in your ad. If she is lacking in any essential, screen out as described in the section below.

Assuming there is nothing disqualifying about your caller so far, you should next ask her an open-ended question. "Tell me a little about yourself—your background, your experience working with children." Of course, you will repeat this question at your interview, in order to see if she tells a consistent story about herself on both occasions. You are well advised to take notes as she describes herself, so that you can keep straight in your mind all the candidates who answer your ad.

As the nanny talks, listen not just to the facts she relates, but to her manner of speaking. Is she articulate? Organized in her account of herself? Able to communicate effectively? Does she sound confident about her abilities or is she hesitant? Is it easy or hard to keep her engaged in conversation?

Assuming she sounds promising over the phone, then go ahead and set up an appointment for an interview in your own home—and be sure to read Chapter Four about interviewing before you do.

Screening Out Techniques. Don't be alarmed if you find yourself needing to screen out a high percentages of your callers. Let's say that in the week after your ad ran in the *Neighborhood Gazette* you got twelve responses. Of all those responses, let's say five of them failed to meet your basic requirements, another four met your requirements but sounded lackluster over the phone, and just three of your callers sounded pretty good. You should set up interviews with these three only, and put all the others off. Here's how:

For the ones who didn't meet your needs, be blunt. *"I'm sorry, but we have to have a licensed driver."* Be specific, if possible: *"You say you've been working in telephone sales for the past year. We really are looking for an experienced nanny, with a recent background in infant care as a full-time job."*

For the ones who seemed qualified, but just didn't give you a great feeling over the phone, leave open the possibility of an interview sometime in the future. Say: *"What we're doing now is simply talking to people over the telephone. When we've had the chance to talk to everyone who has responded to the ad, we'll start calling back to set up our interviews. So let me be sure I've got your name and number correctly, and I will probably be back in touch with you in week or so."*

Save your phone notes on the person as well as the name and number. That way, if the top candidates you interviewed turned out to be disappointing in person, you can indeed go back to some of your other callers and set up more interviews. It could be that one of them does not happen to have a great telephone presence, but is more confidence-inspiring in the flesh. (It could also be that by waiting a week or two, you will get other candidates in response to your ad, and won't need to call the person back—but it's still a good idea to hang on to her phone number just in case.)

Suppose a week or two goes by, and you don't call back any of the also-rans to set up an interview, but one of them calls you back to ask if you are still looking. By this time you have probably interviewed a few candidates and may even be considering hiring one of them. Tell your caller that you may well have found someone, but if it doesn't work out, you may still call them back.

What if you haven't yet interviewed someone who seems good? By all means, consider giving your second-time caller a shot at it. Calling back to inquire about her standing is a good sign on her part: It indicates persistence, a focused approach to her business dealings, and an ability to follow-up in order to meet a goal. Assuming the candidate's second inquiry was politely phrased and came within normal hours, she could be well worth your time for an interview.

One thing you should *never* do is lie to an applicant and say that the position is taken when it isn't. Lying leaves you vulnerable to a charge of unfair employment practices. Imagine what might happen if the caller should discover (by talking with her other friends who are also job hunting) that the job is indeed still available, and that you gave an interview to a subsequent caller. Suddenly that person is driven to wonder, "What is it about *me* that led the employer to turn me away without so much as an interview?" If you haven't given a valid reason, she may start guessing "racial discrimination" or "age discrimination" or some other charge that could lead to an inquiry you don't want to get started. Being truthful and fair to your applicants is your best defense against potential complaints about your hiring practices.

Steps Five, Six, and Seven: Covered in Chapter Four

Step Eight: Check Her Records

Now your potential nanny has passed all your own screening hurdles. You have checked her references (as described in the next chapter) and were impressed with them. You have seen her at work in a lengthy practice babysitting session, and she seemed to do just great.

But you know when it comes to protecting your children, you can never be too careful. The nanny who strikes you as so pleasant, responsible, and dedicated could turn out to be a skillful liar. Her references—especially if they are from far away—could be fake, her whole persona a carefully practiced act. It's unlikely . . . but it's not entirely outside the realm of possibility.

For complete reassurance that she is who she says she is and is not hiding anything nefarious from her past, by all means, have her checked out by a professional investigator.

First, have her sign a release statement giving you permission to obtain her arrest record and her driving record. Appendix C provides a sample statement. In addition, you may also want to have her permission for a standard credit check, to provide you with reassurance that she has a clean financial history: that she is not under any sort of order to have her wages garnished nor does she have any creditors pursuing her (who might harass her at her place of employment, or worse, give her a motive to take what she can grab from your house and disappear).

To find out what investigative services are available to parents, I made an inquiry to a private investigations agency that advertised in a Washington, D.C., area monthly parenting magazine. I spoke to a representative from a company called Search Your Nanny's Past (888-506-Locate), which is a nationwide, licensed, bonded, and insured agency. In response to my request for information, I was promptly faxed a helpful brochure providing me with sample forms and a complete listing of services offered, with prices for each.

The following reports are typically available on an applicant within seventy-two business hours:

> For $39 per jurisdiction: arrest and convictions report ($29 for each extra jurisdiction)
>
> For $39 per jurisdiction: civil records search (to let you know if the applicant has been involved in any civil lawsuits. This may tell you if, for example, she has had any car accidents that did not lead to the filing of criminal charges or points on her license, but for which a civil jury found her at fault, or if she has ever filed a lawsuit seeking damages from a previous employer.)
>
> For $24 each state: validation and history of vehicle operation (driving record)

For $29: financial history, to let you know if she has de-faulted on any of her financial obligations, declared bank-ruptcy, had liens filed against her, has unpaid child support or unpaid taxes, or a history of other financial impropriety.

I learned that a package deal was available for three of these reports for $89, four for $119, or all five for $144.

The investigative agency also offered to do a nationwide search for criminal records for $99. That means for a little over $200 alto-gether you can be assured of an applicant's clean record virtually across the board. For an extra fee you can also check out anyone closely associated with the nanny (since in some cases a husband, live-in boyfriend, or other relative can pose a threat to the family for whom she works).

Although all these fees can mount up, the charge is still far less than what you would pay to a conventional nanny agency—plus, you have the added benefit of personally receiving the reports, rather than having the agency review them and filter the information before pass-ing it along to you.

But is it advisable in every case to hire a professional investigator to do a background check? Sometimes it could well be an unnecessary expense. Here is one such instance:

A young woman who currently works for a neighbor has applied for the position as your nanny. The neighbor, whom you've known and liked for years, and whose judgment you trust, has given the nanny a glowing reference, including vouching for her spotless driving record over the past two years on the job. Before she worked for your neighbor the applicant was a college student who baby-sat for many families in her spare time. Her second reference was provided by a parent for whom she has baby-sat occasionally since she was a high school stu-

If you are thinking about skipping the background check because you intend to use a hidden video camera to record the nanny's performance for the first few days of work, be sure to read the cautions on pages 128–129 in Chapter Five.

dent. Given that you have heard enthusiastic recommendations from two sources who, taken together, can account for the entirety of her working life, there are no gaps to be filled in, no unknowns to be checked out. You can hire the nanny with confidence, and you can save yourself a few hundred dollars by skipping the investigative process.

Here's another situation: You are aware that both of the nanny's previous positions were obtained through an agency, and you know that in order to be represented by that very exclusive agency, the nanny had to have passed the careful scrutiny of the agency's background checkers. Her previous employers have given her wonderful references, so you have no reason to question her *bona fides*.

In some cases, you may not be sure whether you really need a background check or not. My advice is to do what your own level of nervousness makes you feel like doing. If you are the type who likes to have all your *i*'s dotted and your *t*'s crossed, then even when presented with the highest-quality references, go ahead and supplement with a background check—it never hurts. But if you have seen the nanny in several practice babysitting sessions in your home and you feel comfortable and confident that you've sized her up correctly, then you may consider your own positive judgment, combined with her good references, to be sufficient. In that case you may save yourself a few hundred dollars on a private investigator's fee.

DON'T STEAL SOMEONE ELSE'S NANNY

When it comes to stealing, few parents take an absolutist stance. Most of us, if faced with a starving child and no other source of food, would probably say it's not wrong to steal bread for the child's sake. Desperate times require desperate acts.

Some parents seem to view the need for a nanny as justifying theft in a similar way. They act as if there is nothing wrong in approaching a nanny they've observed taking good care of a child and attempting to lure that nanny away from her present employer by means of a better offer. Parents who have had good nannies stolen away are full of outrage when it has happened to them. Parents who currently have great nannies live with the fear that some predatory rich couple may spot their nanny and pounce.

Nothing stops such thievery—it's immoral, but not illegal—except an occasional twinge of conscience on the part of the would-be thieving parents, and the occasional tug of loyalty to the current family on the part of the nanny.

Clouding the ethical picture, too, is the occasional Robin Hoodish aspect of the situation. Sometimes a parent observes a nanny who is obviously overworked and underpaid by her employers. The nanny is doing a terrific job, but her employers don't seem to appreciate what a treasure they've got, and the parents who are hiring her away are simply redressing a basic injustice.

On the other hand, it's often an easy rationalization for thieving parents to use: "Oh, I saw how she was being exploited, and so I offered her an opportunity to escape."

Each of us must live with our own consciences, but my personal rule would be to let the nanny make the first move. You let it be known among the nannies of your acquaintance that you are looking to hire someone, and if someone is unhappy with her present job, let her be the one to come to you. When you recognize that nannies are free agents, capable of making adult decisions, then you understand that her present employer has no "right" to her services; if the nanny chooses to leave her unhappy situation to take your better offer, that's not theft—it's simply the way the free market operates.

Be warned, nonetheless, that the former employer of that nanny is never going to speak to you again!

CHAPTER FOUR

INTERVIEWING AND
REFERENCE CHECKING

The Interview

𝒯he interview is without a doubt the single most important stage of nanny hiring. Qualifications are important, background checks are important, references are important, experience is important—but nothing substitutes for the gut feeling you get from face-to-face dialogue with the person who may get the job.

Based on my own experiences and those of the many parents I interviewed, I recommend making the interview a four-stage process:

Stage One is the **business phase**. You, your spouse, and the nanny sit down in your den or study or somewhere quiet, while a relative or friend looks after your children, and you just talk about the job, adult to adult.

Stage Two is the **walk-through** of your house—her working environment.

Stage Three is the **introduction to your child(ren)**.

Stage Four (assuming you want to go this far with her) is the follow-up or second interview. This one should be a **working interview**. You invite her back to baby-sit for your children for an evening or for a weekend afternoon—or better still, a full day. You pay her for her services for this predetermined block of time, but you don't go out. You stay in the background and observe how she does for the day.

If you like her after all four stages, and she has passed the reference check, which you performed between Stage Three and Stage Four, then you've got your nanny. Hire her!

Stage One: Face-to-Face Talk (Adults Only)

Interview length. Your initial sit-down talk should not be too short. Twenty minutes is never enough time to decide to leave your children with a caregiver. Forty-five minutes should be taken as a bare minimum. If you can't find things to talk about with a nanny for at least that long, then you will certainly have communications problem later on. The only time you should interview for less than the recommended minimum is when you have already decided the candidate is unsuitable and you don't want to waste any more time with her.

Format. Some agencies will give you a list of specific questions to be answered in the interview. In this book I do not provide such a list, because too many parents then go down the list, asking the question, noting the answer, and moving on to the next question, as if giving an oral exam. Such a procedure tells you whether the nanny has been well prepared to be interviewed, not whether she is a decent person who can be counted on in a pinch. To get that sort of sense of her, you need to have the spontaneous give-and-take of a normal conversation. So try to put her at ease, offer her a cup of coffee or tea, settle in, and just talk about the job, your family, your needs, her background, in whatever order seems natural and normal to the flow of your conversation.

Still, have a general plan for some areas of information you want to cover. You don't want to have an aimless, unfocused conversation. You do need to elicit certain facts in the course of the interview. You have already double-checked her history when you called her to set up this chat, and now you need to have her tell in more detail about the kind of families she's worked for in the past, how old their children were, how many, why she left the previous jobs, and what she liked and disliked about nannying in those households.

Give her an overall sense of what working in your home will be like, briefly covering your children's schedules, giving her a sense of how much feedback you expect about their day, what sort of outings she would be expected to arrange, what meals she would be preparing, and what level of neatness you expect. The section below contains some possible discussion points to cover. Turn to pages 87–90 for a few specific questions, including a hypothetical situation for your nanny-candidate to problem-solve.

Some Important Issues to Cover

Discipline. The strategy for introducing this subject is for you to solicit her views before you reveal your own, so that she won't simply be able to nod her head in agreement with you. Mention the variety of techniques that many families practice, including spanking, time-outs, scolding, loss of privileges, and (for babies and toddlers) distraction, and listen to her views on the usage of each, and then compare those views to your own sense of what is effective and right for your children.

Age group preference. It is essential for parents of infants or toddlers still in diapers to discover whether a prospective nanny has an

🕐 DON'T HIRE A SPANKER!

If the nanny tells you that she believes in spanking, bring the interview to a swift conclusion and see her out the door. Even if you personally approve of physical punishment under the proper circumstances, you should beware of the nanny who says she expects to be permitted use of this controversial disciplinary tool. Childcare professionals are nearly unanimous in their belief that spanking is ineffective and even counterproductive in most cases. Even the small minority who support it generally would limit its proper use to parents whose love for the child is beyond question. As a childcare professional, your nanny should be familiar with and confident about the use of many other means of discipline, and should not have to rely upon force to control your child's behavior.

> ⏰ Never hire a nanny who does not have infant experience to take care of an infant and who does not express strong enthusiasm for working with children at this particular stage of development.

affinity for working with very young children, or is more comfortable working with older ones. Some nannies adore babies and are great with them. Others will be wonderfully creative with children of school age but are basically very bored with those who can't talk yet. A few may actually be put off by diapering and all the attendant messes of infancy.

Health and hygiene. Find out about your potential nanny's attitude toward hand-washing: both regarding herself and making the children wash up. Talk about any health problems your children may have. Ask her what she would do if a child developed a fever during the day. In past jobs did she ever take kids to the pediatrician? Does she work when she has a cold? Does she get an annual flu shot? (If not, it's a good policy for you as an employer with small kids to require one—and of course, pay for it).

Schoolwork. If you have children in second grade or higher, you will probably want a nanny capable of supervising them while they do their homework, and perhaps checking to see if it has been done correctly. Certainly parents of all ages of children will want a nanny who is educated at least well enough to read bedtime stories aloud, in a voice expressive enough to sustain their interest.

Driving. If you own a car, I strongly urge you to hire only a licensed driver. Make sure you see her actual driving license and check to be sure it's not expired. You may not need someone to drive your children around regularly, but the ability to drive in an emergency is important. Some cuts and falls are serious enough to require an immediate trip to the pediatrician, but not an ambulance ride. See the section beginning on page 102 in this chapter about how to administer a driving test.

CPR certification. If you listed CPR certification among your requirements, have the nanny candidate tell you where and when she took the course. If it was more than five years ago, you should ask if she's had a refresher course, and if she hasn't, discuss enrolling her in one.

First aid training. Safe nannies are well-trained nannies. In an actual emergency, Louise Woodward panicked and did all the wrong things in the wrong order. Precious minutes were lost that could have been used to save the baby's life. Any nanny candidate who has taken and passed a first aid course should be given preference over an equally good one who has not. You should certainly look into the availability of classes in your area and require enrollment of any untrained nanny you agree to hire. To find a first aid class, try your local hospital, your pediatrician's office, Red Cross chapter, or local "Y." Do not hire any nanny who tells you she is unwilling to take a first aid class.

Nonsmoker. Just have her confirm that she does not smoke—and make clear, if she's a live-in, that you do not allow her guests to smoke in your house, either. I urge all parents, even those who are themselves smokers, to insist upon this rule. Since a nanny should view herself as a childcare professional, and since professionals are expected to hold themselves to a higher standards than the lay people (such as ordinary parents), it is reasonable for you, the employer, to expect your nanny to maintain a smoke-free environment for your children's health.

Work documentation. If the nanny candidate is foreign-born, you will ask to see her "green card," which authorizes her legal residence and employment in this country.

Schedule suitability. Check to make sure she is aware of the days and hours per day that you have listed in your job description, and that she will be able to meet these.

Willingness to perform non-childcare duties. If you are asking for any "extras," such as adult laundry, light housework, or grocery shopping, take some time in your interview to describe the specific tasks you want performed. You need not work out details, such as extra pay for the work, or say how much time she should devote to this or that chore. Save that for the hiring negotiations with the person you eventually select.

Minimum age. Parents of infants and toddlers are wise to prefer an older nanny—one out of her teenage years, at least. Although there are certainly some eighteen- and nineteen-year-olds who can be trusted to exercise good judgment, the safe course is to find an older nanny, whose character has been fully formed, with a long enough employment history to leave a consistent record. Experience has always been the best teacher, and a young girl simply will not have had as much on-the-job learning time as one who has worked full-time for at least five years.

Physical condition. Children have a lot of energy, and it takes a person in good physical shape to keep up with them. If you have a baby, you need to know that the person is strong enough to lift and carry the baby, possibly for a long distance. (Suppose, for example, your nanny took the baby out for a long stroll and a wheel fell off the stroller over a mile from home—you need to be sure she would not be stranded.) With toddlers and older children, the nanny should be able to run faster than the child, and be agile enough to climb to the top of a set of monkey bars, as might be necessary to retrieve her charge when it's time to leave the playground. Because physical demands are part and parcel of the job, you should not accept someone with a heart condition or any other chronic or acute infirmity that limits movement or perception (unless that person has back-up assistance to help them deal with the physical demands described here). Also screen out persons with diabetes or epilepsy, unless the applicant can produce a note from a doctor attesting to the fact that the condition is under control through use of medication and that the person has not suffered from loss of consciousness for a minimum of three years.

Live-in compatibility. When considering sharing your home with a nanny, you need to give yourself at least an extra half hour in your interview just to focus on a wide range of live-in issues. Hiring a live-in is more complicated than hiring a live-out, because you need to concern yourself with aspects of the nanny's private life that would not be relevant, otherwise. Unless the live-in quarters are completely separate and perfectly soundproofed, find out:

- what hours she usually keeps
- TV habits (be sure to ask if likes any late-night shows, and at what volume)
- what kind of music she likes
- her expectations about guests in her live-in residence (including overnight guests of the opposite sex)
- hobbies, interests, and activities in her free time
- what kind of food she likes and dislikes, any special dietary requirements
- her self-described level of neatness
- if she has any specific requests or requirements about the live-in situation

You may have noticed that I have not included a bullet for telephone habits. That is because I *strongly* recommend preventing conflicts over telephone use by offering a live-in her own phone line and answering machine. If you can afford a live-in, you *can* afford a second number! When you draw up your Live-in Agreement, you will probably want to include the stipulation that she pay for her own long distance charges.

See Appendix B for a Live-in Agreement. All families with live-ins should have such an agreement, separate from the Employment Agreement.

Interview Talking Points

The following are some possible discussion points, plus commentary to help you evaluate the candidate's possible responses.

Why does she wants to be a nanny?
Keep in mind: *Everybody* asks this question. Expect an experienced nanny to come back with the standard, correct response: "Because I love children!"

What are her goals for the future?
Keep in mind: Her answer will depend in large part on her age and level of education. A young woman who has completed high school and perhaps some college-level courses will probably have a long-term career goal calling for her to move on at some point in the future to a higher-paid profession. She may be interested in pursuing a career centered around children, such as pediatric nursing or medicine, teaching, or child psychology. Look critically at the young woman whose answer indicates an eagerness to get out of child-centered work altogether, or who seems aimless, without any sense of what her future might hold. An older, professional nanny may tell you that she is content to devote the rest of her life to looking after children—and that's a terrific answer.

Try tossing out the following hypothetical situation:

You have asked the nanny to pick up some groceries for you at the store. After she's filled the cart and is at the check-out line, your two-year-old suddenly launches into a major tantrum. Ask her how she thinks she would handle the situation.

Keep in mind: Her answer does not need to be exactly the same response you would give if you were in that situation yourself. You are mainly looking for some indication that she has experience dealing with tantrums in public and will not get angry or panicky over such behavior. If she answers that she would, first of all, make sure she has finished at the check-out counter before dealing with the tantrum, watch out: That's an indication that she does not have her priorities in order. If she asks for more information about the situation (such as, "Has the child missed his nap?"), that's a good sign. It shows she is flexible, and will look for ways to craft her response to what works best for that individual child. If she stammers and hesitates a long time before speaking, take that as a sign that she has little or no experience to draw from to respond to the question.

Have her name some of her favorite children's books.

Keep in mind: Any nanny who values reading and can communicate that value to your children will have no trouble at all with this question. If she can't come up with at least two or three books off the top of her head, then she's probably not much of a reader. Always make sure the person you hire has a good sense of what sort of books and stories are age-appropriate for your children.

Have her tell you about her best experience in childcare, and then her worst.

Keep in mind: A nanny with sufficient years of experience will have lots of stories to tell. She should have no trouble coming up with something good to say about a past job. Allow her a little time to think carefully about the bad time. Of course, she will want to choose her words carefully. Find out whether the experience she relates was bad because of some difficulty in the employer-nanny relationship, or because of a problem concerning the child. (The former are less of a concern to you than the latter, since presumably your dealings with her will always be fair and above-board.) If the problem stemmed from the child, ask her to tell how (or if) the situation was resolved. That will give you a sense of her ability to cope with problems. If she does not come up with a bad experience to talk about, but shakes her head, and tells you, after a long pause, that she really has never had a bad experience, you might wonder about how honest she will be with you about anything that might go wrong during the normal course of events with your own children.

DISQUALIFIED AT THE DOOR: TWO RED FLAGS

In some cases you can tell from the moment you answer the door that you have a candidate who's not worth the time it takes to interview. If she shows up too late for the interview, you already know she's unreliable. If she shows up dressed in a sexually provocative outfit, you already don't trust her judgment about what's appropriate behavior for an employee.

Lateness. How late is too late? I would allow no more than ten minutes beyond the appointed time. If she phones ahead to let you know she is running late, you may agree to interview her anyway, but be sure she has a valid excuse. Missing a bus or getting stuck in traffic is *not* a good reason for being late. Any responsible person trying to get to an important meeting at an unfamiliar address is supposed to allow sufficient extra time for just such an eventuality. Those who don't call to explain the reason for their lateness should be dismissed with no further chances. This sort of person is likely to forget to call and tell you that she isn't coming in to work on the morning of your bar exam or some other crucial occasion.

Inappropriate appearance. This is a matter calling for personal judgment, as we each have our own individual comfort level for weirdness in dress, makeup, or bodily adornment. My current nanny, for example, sports a nose stud and two tattoos (one, a delicate flower spiraling around her ankle, the other, a rose on her shoulder), but that didn't put me off when I first met her. She is and has always been a wonderfully competent and caring nanny. However, I think I would have drawn the line at a tongue stud or a facial tattoo.

I'm sure I would refuse to interview anyone who showed up dressed in a bustier, or who had on a leather collar or any metal-studded clothing. These are all recognized as overt displays of sexuality. You want your nanny to have a sense of propriety about her person. You do not want her to dress in a way that screams for attention or tries to shock the public at large. These are signs of immaturity.

That said, I would add that the nanny's style of dress after hours should be considered strictly her own business.

Stage Two: The House Walk-Through

Assuming the lengthy talk with your candidate has left you with a favorable impression, the next step is to show her around the place she may call home. As you accompany her through the house, you will be acquainting her with the typical things she will be expected to do in your home each day, pointing out safety features room by room, and familiarizing her with your house rules and practices. The reason to do these things so early in the interview process is to gauge her reactions as you go along. You do not want to hire someone who appears to be puzzled or bored by your descriptions of procedures, nor do you want someone who disagrees with any of your child safety practices. (The tour that follows is written as if for a large house, but of course can be modified to suit the size and layout of your own house or apartment.)

Start on the first floor of your house. Show her where coats are hung, and where muddy kids' boots go on rainy days. Show her the telephone and answering machine and explain your policy about personal calls during the workday. (See the section in Chapter Six for recommendations about safe telephone rules.) Show her your family appointment calendar and explain how you keep each other informed about changes in schedules. Visit the family room, the den, the study, and/or library. Show her the living and dining rooms, making sure that she knows about any parts of the house that are not considered play areas or that you and your spouse would like reserved for your private use. Point out any objects that are off-limits (for example, your personal computer or your collection of antique glass bottles).

Spend ample time in the kitchen. Point out any childproofing devices you have in place (cabinet locks, doorknob covers, refrigerator latch, and/or stovetop shield) and show her how each works. If you lack any of these safety items, explain how she is to prevent your child from accessing certain cabinets, opening certain doors or exploring other dangerous parts of the house. Show her your fire extinguisher—and if you don't have one, get one!

Discuss your children's eating habits and what meals, if any, she will be expected to prepare. Now is a good time to bring up the subject of safe food handling—find out if she knows the basics. (Important rules she should know include: Always wash fruits and vegetables thoroughly. Cook meat and poultry until the juices run clear. Wash cutting boards between uses in hot soapy water. Never serve any food made with raw eggs.) Mention your children's food likes and dislikes. Explain your rules about desserts and between-meal snacks. Mention any foods or beverages that are forbidden. Discuss your children's food allergies or special nutritional requirements. If a child is on medication, describe to your applicant her duties in administering dosages.

For those with babies or toddlers, point out changing tables, potties, play yards, doorway jumpers, strollers, portable cribs, and other pieces of equipment that the nanny will be expected to use safely and at appropriate times. For example, if you have a safety strap on your changing table and want it used at each diaper change, say so. Whether your table has a strap or not, make sure she knows that she is always to keep at least one hand on the child when on the changing table.

Continue your tour of the house, pointing out all smoke detectors that you pass along the way. You should have at least one per floor, ideally with one in each child's bedroom, as well.

Pause in each child's room to point out any tasks you intend for the nanny to handle. Normal duties in this regard include: making the bed(s); keeping the room neat; doing the child's laundry. The nanny might also teach the child to handle these chores on his or her own, when old enough.

If your child naps, discuss the time and the ritual to be followed when putting the child down.

Next visit your own bedroom. Explain any rules you have about children's presence in your bedroom, closet, or bathroom.

If you have attic storage space, make sure the nanny knows how to access it and will observe any safety rules you have about preventing your child's access.

Next, go to the utility area and show the nanny the house circuit breakers or fuses. On this introductory tour you need not go into what to do in case of an electrical problem. Show her where the water cut-off is. If you have a carbon monoxide detector or other safety monitors or alarms, let her see them (though you need not take time to demonstrate how they work). Point out the washer and dryer in the laundry room, but don't spend any time going over your specific washing instructions. Just let her know about how often you expect a children's wash to be done.

If have a playroom or a basement rec room that you expect the nanny to keep straightened up, let her know that as you show her the room.

Next go out to the garage, carport, and/or driveway. Point out the major safety concerns, making clear that children are to be kept out of these areas unless accompanied by an adult.

This part of the tour might be a good time to go over your house security procedures. If you have an alarm system, describe it in general terms—but don't even consider giving out your off-code until the nanny is hired, the Employment Agreement has been signed by all parties, and you are absolutely sure she can be trusted.

Spend a little time in the yard, if you have one. Show her your children's tricycles, bicycles, and other ride-on toys. Let her see the swingset, climbing bars, sandbox, or any other outdoor play structures in your yard.

If you have a pool, make sure she knows how to swim. It is highly desirable for any nanny working in a home with a backyard pool to have taken and passed the Red Cross lifesaving course or some other water-safety class. It is essential that your pool be enclosed by a tall, sturdy fence with a lockable gate, so that a toddler cannot gain access without the aid of an adult. Make sure the nanny knows the number one rule of pool safety: There must always be an adult present when a child is inside the pool fence.

If you have a garden, point out any plants the children are not to touch. Make sure you are well informed yourself about common garden hazards, such as gopher holes; bees' nests; prickly plants such as a cactus, blackberry brambles, and rosebushes; and plants bearing poisonous berries, such as certain hollies.

When outside with the children, the nanny should be instructed to take a cordless phone with her. That way, she will never be tempted to run inside "just for a minute," leaving small children on their own. It only takes a few seconds for a child to dash out in front of a car, or a few minutes to drown in a wading pool.

Each time you describe a particular procedure or cite a safety rule, pay attention to the nanny's reaction; you may receive important clues as to how well you will be able to work with this woman. If she never asks questions but simply nods her head and says "uh-huh" to everything you say, or if she doesn't seem to be paying close attention, that tells you she is a passive personality, and won't contribute her own ideas to your child's upbringing. On the other hand, if she comments on absolutely everything, telling you the way *she* has always handled a situation—especially if she adds something to the effect of: ". . . and I've never had any trouble doing it that way before"—watch out! She may let you think she is following your instructions about keeping your son in your own yard when she is following her own rules, instead. Then one day your next-door neighbor stops by to ask if you wouldn't mind telling your child to stop trampling across the flower beds in her front yard. You ask the nanny if he's been keeping your child within your fence, only to hear her sniff in response: "You are really too overprotective, you know. A five-year-old is certainly big enough to run to a few nearby houses by himself."

The section on monitoring in Chapter Five will tell you how you can effectively check up on your nanny during the first few weeks of employment to discover whether your instructions are being followed; but it is always better to uncover a tendency to such behavior before you hire.

⏰ Do not hire anyone who seems bewildered or bored when you are recounting the safety rules during your house and yard tour.

Stage Three: Meeting Your Child(ren)

Everything seem fine so far? Good. Now bring on the central factor in this equation, the point of all this screening, interviewing, and touring: your child(ren).

Unless your child is an infant (age one or younger) you should introduce the candidate by name. For the time being, you don't need to give any more identification than that. It's premature at this point to bring up the possibility of this stranger becoming an important person in the child's life. Especially if your child is at all shy or hesitant around strange adults, the very mention of a new sitter could set off a crying jag, and you do not want to start things off on a sour note.

Just say, "Nancy [or whatever her name is] is someone I'd like you to meet. She loves to play with little girls [or boys, or both]." Ask your child if she would like to show Nancy her special bear, or whatever object you know she is proud to possess. Or find out if the potential nanny has ever done something you know would be of particular interest to your child. For example, if you have a child who loves dancing, and your interviewee has told you she once took ballet, you could start the introduction this way: "You know Nancy once danced in *The Nutcracker*, just like the show we went to see last Christmas."

Anything you can do to help your child become interested in meeting a new adult will be a plus.

Accompany the child and potential nanny to the child's room or play area. Don't be dismayed if the child figures out pretty quickly that this person is likely to end up as a Mommy substitute—and starts to withdraw, cry, or become clingy. Do observe the nanny's reaction, should any of this behavior occur. If she comes on too strong, is pushy, and insists on trying to pick up a reluctant child, that's a bad sign. On the other hand, if she's entirely too passive, and makes no attempt to engage the child, if she doesn't smile or joke or try to get the child to at least look her way, that spells trouble of a different sort. What you're looking for is a balanced approach—a respect for the child's feelings, coupled with an outgoing, engaging personality. If you find that she's managed to reassure your child or coax her into a happier frame of mind, that's a sign of real talent for the job.

You need to know your own child, too, and give time where more time is needed. Some of the best nannies are utterly rejected in the beginning. (Read "Brenda's Story" below for an example.)

If you're lucky, and you have an outgoing child, he or she will be curious and start talking to the nanny without prompting, and you can sit back and listen. This should be a short session, however, so that your child doesn't get fixated on this one person too early in the process. You still have not checked references, and you might want to interview other candidates, and so you don't want your child to form

---

REJECTION!
THE STORY OF BRENDA

Brenda was a wonderful nanny, but gosh, it took a long time for Annie, who was then eighteen months old, to warm up to her. In the beginning, she ran crying from the room each time Brenda showed up. She was just learning to talk, but she managed to make her feelings clear. "Away, you, away!" she ordered, as Brenda would approach. Fortunately, Brenda was patient and experienced enough to take the situation in stride, and eventually Annie did get used to having her around. I knew things had definitely taken a turn for the better when my husband was roughhousing with Annie over the weekend, and she asked him to "do airplane." He had no idea what she meant. "Airplane, airplane," she repeated, "like Brenda!" He had to call Brenda at home to have her describe the right way to fly Annie through the air.

Many years later, when Brenda was leaving us and Annie was crying over her last good-byes, I reminded her how in the beginning she had not wanted Brenda around. Annie got wide-eyed and denied it was ever possible for her not to have loved Brenda as much as she did now. I started to tell her how she used to scream "Away, away!" but then I realized, it's better for her not to hear that story. She needs to believe that their love was and will always be the same forever, and so I won't tell her anything to contradict her own feelings.

—Lucinda from Long Beach, California

any bonds, before anything is definite. Even if you already love the nanny, the nanny might have reasons of her own not to take the job. Proceeding in slow, deliberate steps is always best for your child's sake.

With an infant or child who does not yet talk, you won't be able to get much out of the first meeting between the nanny and your child. It's perfectly normal for a baby or toddler to scream when being held by an unfamiliar person—or sometimes even looked at closely by a stranger. Of course, an experienced nanny will be aware of this possibility and will not insist on being allowed to pick the baby up.

Assuming the nanny behaves with sensitivity and caution at the meeting with your children, and assuming that she has won your approval in all the previous aspects of the interview, you may now proceed to check her references.

The Reference-Checking Telephone Call

You should be provided with references from at least two separate households in which the nanny has watched children within the past five years. If she has worked for one family, and only one family, for more than five years, then the second family can be one she has worked for on occasional evenings or weekends.

Do *not* accept job references from relatives, friends, other nannies, or anyone who has not been an actual wage-paying employer of the nanny. These others may offer character references that are supple-

---

**RED FLAGS FOR BEHAVIOR DURING THE
INTRODUCTION TO YOUR CHILDREN**

⏰ Do not hire any nanny who barrels in and grabs your baby without waiting for your okay.

⏰ Do not hire any nanny who is so passive that she asks you no questions about your children and, when introduced to them, makes no attempt to engage them in conversation.

mentary in nature, but are no substitute for the observations of real-life employers.

The first thing is to get hold of the references. If you can't get through to a person by the day or evening telephone numbers you have been given after three attempts at each, ask the nanny candidate to give you a different reference. The reference family may be on vacation or on a business trip, so don't hold it against her that you haven't made contact with the first family listed. However, if none of her references seems to be answering their home or work numbers, that's cause for concern. Ask her if she could find out why you have been unable to get through. Be very skeptical about any references that seem to have vanished without a trace (for example, the nanny tells you that her previous employer has moved and she has been unable to track down a forwarding address). You should drop from consideration any candidate for the job whose references cannot be checked.

Let's assume, however, that your call is answered by the person named as the reference. The first thing you do is identify yourself and ask if the person has time to talk to you. If not, arrange to call back at a more convenient time. The very first piece of information you want the reference to confirm is that the family had actually hired the candidate to be a nanny. (See the story in the box on page 99 for the worst that can happen when references aren't adequately checked.)

Hearing that the applicant was a steady worker and a reliable person is not worth much, if the work being praised didn't involve childcare.

You should be sure to find out the ages and number of children cared for. They don't need to match your household exactly—but it is certainly reassuring if they do. That way you can feel confident that the nanny has experience with a family much like your own.

Parents of babies who learn that the nanny's last job was with older children should check to see if she ever did occasional babysitting for other families with infants. It would be very helpful to get one of those parents to provide an additional reference. When inquiring about a nanny's performance with an infant, you may want to ask questions about her handling of specific infant problems, including:

- crying and colic
- diaper changing
- spitting up

> ⏰ Never hire a nanny to care for an infant unless her references confirm that she has been a patient, loving, and enthusiastic caregiver of infants in the past.

- difficulties over feeding
- sleeping and waking at irregular hours
- ear infections and other common pediatric illnesses

Sometimes a person who is enthusiastic and creative with older children will simply lack the patience and gentle touch needed to work with infants. To put it in graphic terms, babies are little fountains of pee, poop, spit-up, and noise. You need to know that your nanny will be able to deal with the constant mess without coming unglued. Beware of words, seemingly complimentary, like "fastidious," "meticulous," or "precise" when applied to someone who will be looking after an infant. Terms like these usually indicate that a person places a higher priority on neatness, order, or schedule-keeping than on making the infant feel loved and secure.

When talking with the reference, converse normally. Just as you did in your interview, you will want to have some general areas to cover in your telephone conversation, but you should avoid reading off a checklist. Your goal is to get the reference to speak candidly and freely about the nanny applicant, not just give some (possibly canned) answers to anticipated questions. So ask open-ended questions, like these two:

"Tell me what you think was her biggest contribution to your children's lives."

"If there was one thing you could change about her, what would it be?"

Do pay close attention to the specific adjectives the reference chooses to describe the nanny. Most people want to be helpful to former employees and so will be reluctant to say anything negative—even if it's relevant to the question under consideration. Instead, they fall back on certain all-purpose terms of praise to draw focus away from potential areas of concern. "Sweet," for example, is a rather empty description that may cover up a multitude of sins. A person can be sweet, but lack judgment, brains, or maturity. If you don't hear praise of her intelligence or common sense, be sure to ask: "Would you also describe her as smart?"

Probe more deeply if the reference lays greatest emphasis on the applicant's enthusiasm or energy level. One can be full of great plans and creative ideas, but not careful in the least about how to implement them. Make sure you get an appraisal of the applicant's attention to detail, concern for safety, and ability to supervise adequately.

Of course, you'll ask the reference for an opinion about punctuality, reliability, and overall trustworthiness.

As the reference talks, listen not just to what is said, but what is *not*

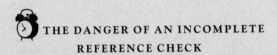

THE DANGER OF AN INCOMPLETE REFERENCE CHECK

Of all the tragedies involving infant death while in a sitter's care, the one I remember best was an incident that happened close to my own home in Washington, D.C., to a family who were members of the same congregation as my family. The parents, both attorneys, had hired someone to look after their three-month-old baby full time. Of course the mother had called to check the person's references. The previous employer told her that the candidate had been a good worker and had always been very reliable. What the reference neglected to mention was that the person had done only housecleaning for her, never childcare. The parents did not do any more checking. If they had done a background check, they would have discovered that their nanny had served time in prison for forgery. Her true history came out too late—it was in the newspaper account published after the nanny had been arrested and charged with causing the baby's death. At the time, my own baby was a newborn, and I had not yet thought about hiring a nanny—but the facts of the case remained fixed in my mind long afterward, and definitely had an impact on the time and attention I gave to reference checking when I became a nanny employer myself.

being said. Watch out for any hesitation or long pauses before answers to questions emerge; that could indicate the reference may be choosing her words a bit too carefully, not wanting to reveal her doubts to you. If that is the case, try to draw the person out. Say: "I'm sensing some hesitation. Is there some reservation you have, or maybe something that occurred that may make you a little bit cautious on this nanny's attitude in this particular area?" If the response is "No, no, I'm one hundred percent confident of her abilities," then you can move on to the next issue.

But in some cases you just might draw out of the reference an anecdote that will make you aware of some flaw in the nanny's history or character. Then it's up to you to decide which of three courses to follow:

1. Investigate the matter further, to determine if the nanny has learned from her mistake and changed for the better.

2. Consider the mistake a trivial one, and disregard it as a factor in your hiring decision.

3. Rethink your intention to hire based on the reference's information.

Should you receive a less-than-glowing report from a reference for a nanny who in all other regards has impressed you most favorably, it may be worth your while to discuss the reference's report with the nanny and hear her side of the story. If, after your talk with her, you feel completely reassured by her explanation for the reference's lack of approval, go ahead and hire—but be especially vigilant about the spot-checks you perform during her first two weeks of work. (Spot-checking is described in detail in Chapter Five.)

The trouble is that there is no set formula for evaluating a reference's appraisal of a nanny. You listen carefully for nuances; you hope you've covered all the bases; you get back in touch with the nanny regarding any problematic tales you've heard—but none of that is much of a guarantee of safety in the end.

The next step in the process, however, will give you as clear a sense of the nanny's value as you are ever going to be able to get before hiring.

Stage Four: The Follow-up Interview

If you've come this far, you are probably already well-disposed to your candidate and are thinking you might hire her. This final stage of the interview process should give you the ultimate confirmation of the rightness of that decision—but it also could save you from making a hard-to-correct mistake. Call your candidate back for a second interview—but make clear that after an initial ten- or fifteen-minute chat, her visit will segue into an actual babysitting session with your kids.

Make clear to her that you will be paying for her time at a standard rate. Look to set up this working interview on a weekend during the day or over an evening weeknight or two—but try to arrange at least three hours in a row when your children will be awake. Longer is better, and if you can arrange for your candidate to work all day for both days of the weekend, that will really give you a very complete idea of what she'll be like as your full-time nanny.

You should not leave the house during the practice session but remain nearby, so that you can at least hear any loud sounds that may be produced. You may, however, want to give your children the impression that you have gone out, so that they will turn their attention to the sitter and not continue to look for you around the house.

Prepare your children in advance for having a new sitter for this particular day or evening. You might want to consider supplying the nanny with some sort of treat to give to your kids upon arrival. Yes, of course it's a bribe, and bribery in the long run is a bad parenting technique, but if it works to smooth the path of acceptance on this special occasion (and you don't resort to bribery too often), why not use it?

When the nanny comes, first spend a little time chatting with her, just to be sure your initial impression of her hasn't changed. You might give her a refresher tour of the areas of your house where your children will be playing, eating, or napping. If she will be preparing the children's lunch or dinner, let her know what food you'd like her to make, and give her any other special cooking instructions she may need.

Be sure to go over any specifics of your children's care, such as medications, allergies, favorite "blankies," and other subjects she will need to know to handle their care for the time she's there. Give the nanny extra credit if she has remembered any or all of the childcare information you imparted at your first meeting. Then, after picking an appropriate moment when the children seem to be at ease and comfortable with the idea of your going away for a while, retire to another part of the house and busy yourself with some project or other, all the while keeping one ear cocked for any indication of trouble.

If the nanny is as good as you've been hoping she would be, you will not have to put in an appearance for hours. In that case, you've found the right person, so go right to Chapter Five and read up about your negotiations to hire. As soon as the babysitting day comes to an end, you will want to make her an offer, so that you won't let any more days pass by during which she may be interviewed and be accepted elsewhere.

If she seems just so-so during the practice babysitting session, continue to interview and check references, without ruling her out entirely. Then, after you've had enough time to see a few other candidates in action, you can go with the one you think is the best of the lot . . . or decide to keep looking, and perhaps expand your search beyond the means you've used so far.

The Driving Test (Optional)

Many parents need a nanny in large part because they need a children's chauffeur. The children may be of school age and old enough to be left on their own, but they still need an adult to drive them to their different schools, pick them up at various times, and take them to their lessons, doctor's appointments, after-school programs, friends' houses, and other destinations. Driving, for these families on the go, is the most important skill. In such a situation, it will not be enough to simply check the nanny's driving record to be sure that she has never had her license revoked or suspended.

The parents need to be shown that the nanny is safe behind the wheel of the particular vehicle they own—especially if the parents own something oversized or hard to maneuver, such as a sport utility vehicle or a minivan. Families who live in colder climates need to be reassured about the nanny's ability to drive in snow. Where terrain is rough or conditions difficult, families will also want to see the nanny in action.

In that case, the parents should require a test drive. Either you or

🕐 Do not hire anyone who would violate any posted driving rules while on a test drive with a potential employer! Accept *no excuses!*

your spouse should go out with the nanny at the wheel, and the parent in the front passenger seat. Check to see if she adjusts the mirrors and buckles her seat belt properly before she takes the car out of park.

First, direct her to drive along the routes she will be most commonly using in her employment with you: to school, to playgrounds and parks around the neighborhood, to the grocery store, and to the doctor's office.

After you've covered a few common, nearby destinations, have her get on the highway and go for a couple of exits. Observe how she merges and changes lanes. Does she signal each time? Is she keeping to the posted speed limit?

Observe her attitude. Is she paying close attention to her driving or is she chatty and offhanded about the test drive? Does she seem anxious and overly fearful about having an accident? Both overconfidence and overanxiousness are causes for concern.

Can she parallel park? Can she back out of a long, winding driveway cautiously and correctly? Can she put your car into your garage without scraping the fenders? Be sure to put her through all of the paces that any driver of your children would be likely to have to perform as part of a normal day's routine.

Be especially careful to instruct her in the proper way to secure your infant or toddler carseat or booster into your back seat. Car accidents are the number one killer of small children in this country, and a child may be as much at risk in an improperly installed carseat as one who is not restrained at all. (For more information about car safety, see the section on that subject in Chapter Seven.)

If at any time during the test drive you find yourself feeling dubious about her attention to safety or her ability to handle your vehicle, you may choose one of three courses of action:

1. Because she is so impressive in all other respects, hire her anyway, and restructure the job so that driving is no longer required. There

are licensed and bonded child transportation services you can use instead. (Try looking in your telephone directory under "Taxi" for a service with a name like SafeRide, KidTaxi, or something in a similar vein.)

2. Hire her conditionally, but send her to a professional driving school so that she can take a course in the particular road skills you require. Don't let her drive your children until she has been certified by the instructor as well qualified and safe. Of course, you should offer to pay for the course. Such a condition may prove an excellent solution when the nanny is basically a careful driver but is simply unfamiliar with American driving patterns because she is a recent immigrant from the United Kingdom, Jamaica, Ireland, or any other part of the world where people drive on the left.

3. Keep looking for a nanny who inspires your complete confidence behind the wheel.

Two Cardinal Rules for All Employers of Nannies

The two most important rules of nanny hiring are as follows:
1. *Allow sufficient time for a thoroughgoing search and*
2. *Always have a back up plan.*

How Much Time Is Enough?

Choosing a nanny is a bit like choosing a spouse (and the consequences of choosing badly can be much the same—a split that can be nearly as time-consuming and emotionally draining as a divorce.) If, after the lengthy, multistep process described here, you are still not sure, *hold off*! Do not commit! When the right one comes along, you'll know. You will feel confident and happy and ready to grab her and make her part of your life.

The problem is, for too many parents, there is far too much pressure to find someone—anyone—and so be able to get back to a normal work schedule. But just like the teenage girl who succumbs to social pressure to find a boyfriend—any boyfriend—the relationship formed under such pressure will seldom be good for the long haul.

Since a nanny hired in haste due to workplace pressures may need to be replaced, also in haste, it will be worth your while to invest the necessary time in searching the first time out. That may make your work life a bit more difficult for a while: You may need to put off crucial meetings, beg for extensions on project due dates, and juggle your hours to make time for your nanny interviews. You may worry about appearing as if you're on the "Mommy Track" rather than the fast-track—but at least, if you do it right, you won't have to go through the hiring process again for a long, long time.

One possible solution, is of course, for Dad to do his fair share of the nanny-hunting and child-minding in the interim, rather than leave most of the chore in Mom's hands. Indeed, a few of the couples I interviewed made a point of equal participation in the childcare duties until the best replacement could be found.

The reality for the vast majority of couples, however, is that coping during the period without a nanny falls mostly on the mother. And if the nanny she selects should turn out to be a poor choice, she generally ends up with the blame for that as well. Bosses (usually male) may not want to hear your woes. If you are out for too many days because of your childcare needs, they wonder if you are committed to your job. But then if you hire your first applicant so that you don't have to miss any work, you may end up needing to take a leave of absence anyway, to deal with your hiring mistake—and you're no better off in your boss's eyes than you were before.

To prevent yourself from falling victim to this sort of pressure, I recommend giving yourself a minimum of eight to twelve weeks to complete the nanny-hiring process. Ideally, you would get your spouse to commit to take time off from work as well. To make sure that you're not just getting lip service to the idea of equal time, see to it that he blocks out the needed time on his calendar.

Parents of newborns, who have no experience in hiring, might be well advised to give themselves up to another month to explore their childcare options. If maternity leave is only six weeks, that means that the parents should get to work on the search before the end of the second trimester of pregnancy.

Why Make a Backup Plan?

There may come a time when you have no warning that you'll be needing a new nanny. You may find yourself in a situation in which your current nanny quits, or suddenly becomes incapable of working, or does something that leads you to have to fire her on the spot. That doesn't mean you have to hire in haste! Every safety-minded parent needs to have a backup plan for childcare for just such contingencies. You need this even when you already have the best nanny in the world, for what will you do if she suddenly has an accident, or falls seriously ill, and can't work anymore?

Each couple needs to look at their own situation and figure out their own best method of coping. Plan to cover your childcare needs for eight to twelve weeks at a minimum, so that you won't have to cut corners on your search.

To come up with a suitable plan, you might:

- consider how your job(s) could be restructured to allow you to work out of your home
- consider whether one or both of you could arrange to take an extended leave of absence or a sabbatical
- investigate day-care centers to see if one could serve as your stop-gap provider
- recruit a trustworthy temporary nanny to agree to be your stand-by. This might be a close relative who would step in for free, a stay-at-home neighbor who might like to earn some extra money, or another nanny who might be willing to take part in a short-term share arrangement for added pay

If you're not convinced of the need to draw up a contingency plan, just think back to the last time you saw one of those horror stories on the news about a child who was found to have been abused by a nanny. As a microphone is shoved in the mother's face and she's asked why she hired the nanny, doesn't she always respond with something to this effect: "I had some doubts about her from the first, but then . . . I *had* to go to work."

Only too late comes the realization that you also *have* to protect your child—and that is far more important.

CHAPTER FIVE

HIRING AND FIRING

Making Your Choice

ou've completed your interviews and your candidates' driving tests, you've checked out their references, and you've received the all-clear from the background checking agency. At the end of this road you find yourself thinking along one of the following three lines:

A. You are very enthusiastic about your top candidate.

B. You feel your top candidate is probably okay, but you were hoping to find someone you could really get excited about . . . and she isn't it.

C. You are not really satisfied with any of the nannies you met during the process.

If either A or C describes your feelings accurately, your next move is clear: If it's A, then make her an offer (and proceed to page 109 of this chapter). If it's C, go back to Chapter Two, Using an Agency, or Chapter Three, Hiring Independently, and repeat the steps. You may want to consider switching methods, as well. If you let an agency conduct your search the first time around, this time try doing it on your

own; if you couldn't come up with anyone great on your own, now try
to find the very best agency to assist you.

We're left with those who answered B. If you gave yourself ample
time to search, you should still have some time to spare, and so should
probably keep on looking, until you come up with someone you feel is
better than just "okay." You want to be positively enthusiastic about
the nanny who will take care of your children.

Try to focus on what might have been lacking in your search efforts
the first time around. Think about your notices. Perhaps they were a
little dull? This time, see if you can jazz them up a little, use some
color, or add a splashy graphic to catch the eye of a passerby. If, after
a second round of interviews and reference checks, you are still not
thrilled with anybody who has responded so far, see if you can identify
any problem intrinsic to the job itself:

- Are you offering too low a salary to attract good candidates?
- Are your hours too long or unpredictable?
- Is your location too remote?
- Is your live-in space too austere?
- Are you asking for more housework than a typical nanny is
  expected to perform?
- Is your household run by too many rules and schedules, leaving
  little room for the nanny's own creative input?
- Are you turning down otherwise good candidates because of
  problems that may be solvable? (For example: Your best nanny
  candidate said she couldn't work on weekends, so you did not
  hire her, because you wanted someone who could work a half-
  day on Saturdays.)

During your third (and hopefully final) round of posting notices
and placing ads, you can make an effort to overcome these problems by:

- offering the highest possible salary you can afford without busting
  your budget. (If your best offer is still on the low side of what
  good nannies in your region usually earn, then start checking out
  those day-care centers and shared-nanny situations.)
- altering your work schedule to fit in better with the hours provided by the average full-time nanny. If you can't manage to

reduce your hours to what a single caregiver would be likely to cover, then perhaps you could hire a second, part-time nanny to provide the overtime you require.

- offering the nanny a transportation subsidy (money for gasoline or busfare), so that it won't be too expensive for her to commute to your remote location.
- spending what it takes to make your live-in space as attractive and comfortable as possible. If the space cannot be substantially improved, then look for nearby rentable space to provide the residence your new nanny requires.
- rethinking some of your rules and schedules that may overly restrict the activities and outings a creative nanny would choose for your child.
- making compromises and adjustments necessary so that you can hire an otherwise excellent nanny, who for one reason or another, cannot accept the job as initially offered. To stick with the example introduced above, here is a possible solution to the problem of the nanny who could not work on weekends: You simply find a neighborhood college student or other part-time sitter who could fill in for the nanny during those desired Saturday mornings.

The main thing is, don't give up too soon. With a little persistence, creativity, and flexibility on your part, you *will* be able to find the nanny you want. She *is* out there!

Making the Offer

First a little sweet talk, just to start things off with a smile. Tell the nanny you want her to know how impressed you have been with her. Tell her how much you are looking forward to having her as your children's nanny. Then get down to business. And get it down in writing. Present her with an employment agreement that spells out her employment terms, her duties, and your obligations, and give her some time to look it over. If necessary, set a date for her to come back and talk about any changes or clauses she would like to have inserted; then each of you sign on your respective dotted lines. See Appendix A for the Sample Employment Agreement.

If the nanny will live in, have her sign a separate Live-in Agreement. The sample Live-in Agreement is Appendix B.

Take a look at these documents, but don't just copy them: Tailor them to suit your family's and your nanny's individual needs and preferences. Just be sure you have given due consideration to all the issues discussed in the sections that follow.

You don't need to hire a lawyer to review your written agreements. The purpose of having a written agreement is simply to prevent misunderstandings between you and the nanny, by spelling out each party's rights and obligations in clear and simple language. These agreements will not give you an airtight defense in the event of a lawsuit, because given our society's present state of litigiousness, nothing will. As we've seen in far too many cases, no matter how many lawyers go over the fine print, no matter how many clauses and conditions you throw in, people can always sue . . . and they frequently do. The worst part about it is that from time to time a plaintiff with an off-the-wall claim will end up with an equally off-the-wall jury, and win. The message in such victories is that you shouldn't agonize over the wording of your Employment Agreement, because an offended person can always invent a breach of contract out of nothing.

Your best defense against legal hassles comes from prevention. All that screening you did in advance of hiring (you hope!) has kept you from taking on anyone of a litigious bent.

Negotiating Pay and Benefits

Suppose you've put forward your best offer . . . but the nanny wants something a little more than you were prepared to give. If you really, *really* want her, be prepared to compromise. The following are the main topics of negotiation, with some examples of conflicts and some suggestions for resolution.

The Basic Pay Package

Salary. You should always start out offering a pay rate somewhat below what you could actually afford if you stretched your budget. That way you have some leeway to meet her asking price. If her salary demand is equal to what she made from her previous employer, then she has a good case that she's worth the money. On the other hand, if her salary demand is way above what you know other similarly qualified nannies are receiving in your area, go ahead and point that out. Whatever comes out of the negotiations, you should try not to let any tension that has developed over the money issue negatively affect your developing relationship. Business is business, and a good nanny will protect herself financially, just as any smart and assertive person would in any other field. If anything, her hard-headedness in negotiating her salary should tell you that you have found a nanny with some business sense, plus a good deal of confidence in her own worth.

Overtime. The standard rate in most other jobs, time and a half, is definitely too much for most parents to afford. Many parents never pay *any* overtime; they consider the weekly salary to cover an approximate rather than exact number of hours per week. If they happen to come home an hour early one day, then the nanny can take off early without being docked any pay; if the parents happen to come home an hour late the next day, the nanny will work the extra hour, without an additional hour's pay. The key to preventing conflict is to make sure everyone understands and accepts this arrangement; and that overtime hours are repaid by equal hours off. Whenever possible, the nanny should be given advance warning of changes in schedule to be able to adjust her own plans.

If the nanny does not accept such informal trading of hours, then you will have to negotiate a rate for overtime pay. My suggestion would be to come up with an hourly rate based upon what you pay for an occasional evening babysitter.

Payment for long blocks of overtime, such as a full weekend of babysitting while you and your husband are out of town, are a different matter altogether. You should give the nanny at least a few weeks notice of your travel plans and then offer a flat fee for the time required. If you were to pay by the hour, a forty-eight-hour weekend would probably run you over $300 (since responsibility for the children doesn't end just because they are asleep at night); but the parents I interviewed who had negotiated for a full weekend's work were paying in the neighborhood of $150 to $250 for the time.

Health coverage. Some nannies will opt for a smaller base rate of pay in exchange for substantial benefits. Health insurance is usually the costliest one that may be required—and in my opinion very worthwhile for the employer, as much as for the nanny. Just think what would happen if your now-healthy nanny were to break her leg, or need her appendix taken out? Who would pay her hospital bills? When she appealed to you for help, could you turn her down? A call to your family's insurance agent will get you the information you need about rates for a no-frills policy that covers "major medical" costs. With a large deductible, the premiums will be surprisingly affordable—perhaps as low as $65 a month. You may want to negotiate for the nanny to split the payments equally with you, or pay some other portion of the bill.

The Resource Guide in the back of this book lists a toll-free number for an insurance agency that serves as the official representative of the International Nanny Association, and provides low-cost policies covering both short-term and long-term nannies.

Time Off

Vacations. The normal practice of employers in this country is to insist that a certain term of employment be completed before paid vacation days are earned. A reasonable formula would be to allow one week, or five working days, of paid vacation to accumulate per each six-month block of time the nanny has worked for you. For her to build up a two-week paid vacation (ten working days) she would need to have worked for you for a full year.

Other days off. This is where the nationality of your nanny can really count. A nanny born and brought up in the United States will probably expect to get all our national holidays, including the minor ones like Presidents' Day, Columbus Day, and Veterans Day. She may negotiate as well for the day after Thanksgiving, and the week between Christmas and New Year's Day. Foreign-born nannies are more likely to accede to your request to consider all of those days as part of their normal work schedule, but they will still expect, and should certainly receive, all the major American holidays such as Thanksgiving, Christmas, the Fourth of July, Martin Luther King Jr.'s Birthday, Labor Day, and Memorial Day. In addition, you may be asked to give the nanny time off on days of religious or cultural significance to her, such as Good Friday, Bastille Day, or Boxing Day (the day after Christmas in most British Commonwealth countries).

Sick days. Five days of paid sick leave per year is a reasonably generous offer. Some employers will wait until they have had a nanny for six months to a year before offering any payment for the time she's out sick. That way they can get a sense of the nanny's overall health and her attitude toward sickness, and become assured that if they offer some paid sick days, she won't take advantage and stay home over minor matters. If the nanny ends up needing more than five days per year, the extra days may be upaid, and if the total per year is more than ten days, you may want to reevaluate her ability to hold the job. Only a basically healthy person should be working as a nanny.

Unpaid leave. Family emergencies and important events, such as a funeral, a wedding, or the birth of a sister's child, may call the nanny away with little notice. Most employers will deal with the problem on a case-by-case basis, but it's always helpful to have a policy in writing to apply to the situation. You and the nanny can always renegotiate and initial any changes in your agreement as the circumstances warrant. You may write down a specific number of days that may be taken as unpaid leave without jeopardy to the nanny's position, or you may simply wish to note that any days taken other than those specified holidays and sick days must be cleared first with you and will be uncompensated. Although the nanny will not be able to promise to give a specific amount of notice for her unpaid leave, you should make clear to her that you expect to be told about any leave of absence as soon as possible, to allow you time to arrange for fill-in childcare.

Maternity policy. You need not write a maternity policy into your agreement, but can craft your response when the time comes. However, you might want to do a little thinking on the subject ahead of time, just in case the nanny brings it up herself during the negotiations. If she is married and has been considering starting a family, she may be looking for a job that would allow her to include care for her own baby in the arrangement. There are many considerations to be taken into account by such a prospect (more than I have space to cover here) and you are well advised to take some time to explore them carefully before you respond to such a request.

Other Benefits to Consider

Payment of employment taxes. If your nanny is legal, you should certainly be filing and paying your share of employment taxes. By doing so, you will avoid serious trouble with the IRS, keep your reputation for above-board business practices in your own community, and as an added benefit, be eligible to receive the government's childcare tax credit. The question is: Should you be paying the nanny's share as well? Many nannies will expect you to. It's not an inconsequential sum of money—but not enough to be a deal-breaker, either. If you want to hold firm on the issue, you may want to offer as a substitute a nice annual bonus, since bonuses are exempt from payroll taxes.

Raises. After your nanny has been with you a year and you have sat down with her and confirmed that she will continue to work for you through the coming year as well, it's standard for you, as her employer, to increase her pay. For example, if she started out making $325 a week, add $25 a week to take her up to $350. If $325 was already near your limit, then see if you can manage to go to $330. Anyone who has done a good job taking care of your kids for over a year really does deserve a raise—and you'd be well advised to factor in the anticipated annual increases when you set her starting salary. Remember as you increase her pay to get out the Employment Agreement and change the specified salary listed and have the change initialed by all parties.

Personal use of a car. If the nanny doesn't have her own car she may ask to have occasional, or perhaps even exclusive, use of a car that you own. In many of our cities and suburbs where driving is a way of life (especially in California and other western states), the nanny may even turn down any job that does not include such a benefit. It is probably best at the outset not to make any promises about car access in your written agreement, but wait until at least the end of the probationary period, after she has earned your full confidence behind the wheel. If, at the end of that time, you don't trust her enough to let her borrow your car from time to time, you certainly should not be trusting her with your children full-time, and should fire her. Just make sure she knows to leave the car with a full gas tank when she's done. You may ask her to pay for the gas she uses up herself—but the more generous position is to reimburse her for the fill-ups. Make it clear that only she (not her boyfriend or anyone else) is permitted to drive, and that if she has had any alcohol at all (even one beer) you do *not* want her behind the wheel.

Housing subsidy (for live-out). Suppose your top candidate was really hoping for a live-in position; you really want to hire her, but you just don't have the room. Consider offering her a housing subsidy. Subsidies can be direct (you simply pay her an additional sum equal to her rent) or indirect (you find her a suitable place to live and you pay the landlord yourself). A subsidy need not be total; you could always negotiate for her to pay a certain portion of her monthly housing costs herself.

Food. I have heard stories about families who tried to restrict what the nanny ate during working hours, or who declared certain types of food off-limits. This strikes me as a miserly sort of attitude, sure to cause the nanny offense. My recommendation would be to give your nanny full access to the refrigerator. Perhaps under special circumstances, such as when you have prepared a dish for a dinner party, you might request that she leave that dish alone. If you find that you are always running out of something she consumes—soda, perhaps, or milk—just ask her to take note of when supplies are getting low, and pick up some more at the store. She should, of course, be reimbursed for any food that the whole family consumes.

Negotiating Duties

You have already specified in your job notice or description to the nanny agency the main childcare duties you require. All other tasks not related to childcare may be up for negotiation. A few of these are:

Housework. Most nannies will clean up after the children in their care without complaint. However, many nannies are asked by their employers to do much more—and those nannies usually don't like it! Parents are warned that they should seek the nanny's agreement if they want any of the following: dusting, vacuuming, straightening up of rooms other than a child's bedroom or playroom, making the parents' bed, doing the parents' laundry, cooking for the whole family, doing the dishes after the family's meals, and cleaning bathrooms. You should not expect to get a full-time housekeeper and nanny for the price of a single employee, so be prepared to pay extra for any of these extra chores.

Pet care. First make sure before hiring that the nanny has no allergy to or phobia about any of the pets you may have. A nanny's responsibility regarding pets is usually limited to the care of any small pets belonging your child that live in a cage in your child's bedroom. Gerbils, hamsters, mice, small birds, frogs, newts, and goldfish are common examples. A good nanny will teach your children how to care for their own pets as soon as they are old enough to do the job correctly.

Larger pets (mainly dogs and cats) are not part of the standard arrangement, but if it is your intention to include pet care in the list of duties, you should certainly have brought up the subject during your interviews and excluded any candidates who would not oblige. As with housework, you probably will have to pay extra for time-consuming tasks such as dog-walking or cat-litter cleaning. A nanny should never be asked to take on any aspect of pet care involving danger (for example, training an aggressive dog not to bite, or giving a cat a bath) or specialized skills (such as administering medication to a pet).

Yardwork. Don't ask the nanny to rake your leaves, shovel your walk, paint your tool shed, dig your fence posts, or plant your annuals. She's your children's caregiver, not your neighborhood day-laborer. Of course, if she should happen to hear you sighing about how hard it is to find reliable help to perform any of these tasks, she just might offer her services for a reasonable price. In that case, strike a deal!

Grocery shopping. Few nannies object to being asked to pick up supplies now and again for the family. Many will agree to do the weekly shopping, as well, since a large percentage of what goes in the cart will be for the children's meals. Still, you should not just assume that she will take on the task; it's always wise to discuss an issue before you write it into your list of regular duties. Payments made for groceries should always be reimbursed.

Travel with the family. You have already informed the nanny during her interview that she may be required to travel with the family.

Make sure she holds (or has applied for) a passport before arranging any trips abroad. You need not specify in your Employment Agreement what the compensation for each trip shall be—you can work that out once you know the destination, length, and schedule of the trip. As a courtesy to your nanny, allow her as much notice as possible so that she may arrange her personal schedule around your travel plans. Remember, when nanny travels with you, it is work for her, not a vacation, and treat her time accordingly. Make sure that she receives sufficient time off each day to prevent burn-out. During a long trip of a week or more, she will need at least one full day off. Of course you pay for her airfare, her accommodations, and her meals.

Three Non-Negotiable Issues

Sometimes you set the policy unilaterally, and the nanny must either take the package or leave it. That should be the case when it comes to the following three issues:

1. giving the nanny notice of termination
2. requiring notice from her of her intention to quit
3. establishing the rules of the probationary period

Let's take them one at a time.

Giving Notice

The last thing you want to have in your home is a nanny who is upset or angry over being fired, but who has to work for two more weeks while you interview replacements right under her nose. The only sure way to prevent such an emotionally trying circumstance from arising is to provide *no notice* for termination. Have her job end on the same day she learns that you no longer want her services. To keep things even-handed (since, as per the paragraph below, you will be requesting at least two weeks notice from her when she is the one who wants out)—you should present her with two weeks salary as severance pay at the same time that you tell her you are letting her go.

**IMPORTANT RULE: ONCE YOU'VE FIRED,
GET THEM OUT!**

One of the most common and dangerous mistakes parents make is to keep a fired nanny working until her replacement can be found. This can be a recipe for tragedy, as the old nanny, feeling embittered and misused, takes out her hostile feelings on the employer's helpless children. Learn from the headlines, and *don't do it.* Fire, and have the untrustworthy nanny depart the same day. Use your backup plan for childcare in the interim. (See page 106 on the necessity, for safety's sake, of an eight- to twelve-week backup childcare plan.) This rule could save your child's life!

In certain circumstances you should not offer any severance pay. A nanny who has acted recklessly or abusively toward your children deserves nothing except the boot. Examples of such conduct include:

- leaving your child(ren) unattended in the house or in a car for any length of time (even two minutes)
- hitting, slapping, dragging, shoving, or otherwise mistreating your child(ren)
- theft (for which you have credible evidence)
- drinking or using illegal drugs on the job
- reckless driving or other serious misuse of your car
- lying about her background as it affects her qualifications for the job

Requiring Notice

How much warning should you ask to be given of the nanny's intention to leave your employment? Your Employment Agreement should stipulate a minimum of two weeks notice of her intention to leave . . . but that said, don't count on it. No matter how stern the wording of this clause in your Employment Agreement, you will have no way to enforce it. During my interviews for this book I heard story after story of the nanny who departed in the night without so much as a hint to the parents that something was wrong. Your best hope of getting advance word of your nanny's plans to depart will come from your having built up a warm, open, trusting relationship with her. That way, when she is considering moving on in life, she will let you know of the possibility long before it is a settled matter, and if you are lucky, she may even consult you on the timing of her plans.

The Probationary Period

It is very important for your Employment Agreement to lay out a period of time for you, your children, and the nanny to get used to each other, to be sure that you've made a good match. Probationary actually means "trying out" or "testing," which accurately describes what the period allows, but because the term is used more commonly in the criminal courts to describe a person allowed to remain free under strict supervision, you might prefer to use a gentler euphemism in your Employment Agreement. Try "evaluation period," "training period," or simply "trial period."

Make clear to the nanny that the "see-how-it-works-out" provision is mutual, so that either one of you is free to call it quits within the time specified, without penalty or delay.

How long should that time be? If you hired through an agency, you won't have the freedom to determine the length yourself. Your agency contract will tell you exactly what date your fee becomes nonrefundable, after which no more replacements will be provided. Some give you thirty, some sixty, and the generous agency may give you up to ninety days to make a change without penalty.

When you hire independently you can decide for yourself how long you think you'll need to get a clear sense of your satisfaction with the nanny's work. In general, longer is better—so give yourself up to three months, if the nanny will agree.

Tips and techniques to help you accurately assess the nanny's performance during the probationary period are discussed in the section titled "Spot-checking" starting on page 123.

Negotiating the Live-in Agreement

When safety is your first priority you want things arranged such that you are never bound to keep on someone you have concluded is not to be trusted around your children. For this reason you must craft your Live-in Agreement so that the nanny will vacate your premises as soon as her job with you has ended. The best thing is to have the probationary clause in your Live-in Agreement mirror the time period laid out in your Employment Agreement. Make sure the nanny has a back-up plan for prompt change of residence during that time period, so that she can move out the same day (or fairly soon thereafter) if either she or you has decided to end her employment. Otherwise your nanny could end up with no job, no prospects, and no place to live but your house—and it will be costly for you (both legally and emotionally speaking) to evict her.

If an agency has arranged to bring the nanny to you from outside your area, let it be up to agency to deal with her return flight or accommodations in the event of termination. But be warned: The time to have addressed these issues was before you signed the agency contract. If you are reading this because you want to know what to do after the fact, I'm sorry, but the answer is: not much. Just pay her return airfare and vow not to make the same mistake again.

Once you have reserved for your side the all-important right to

IMPORTANT LIVE-IN SAFETY RULE!

⏰ Never allow a nanny to move into your house unless you are sure there will be someplace she can go (and that she *will* go) if things don't work out.

require her departure upon termination, be liberal about the comforts and privacy she may expect for her part of the bargain.

Agree that her room is her private domain, and that she may keep it as she likes. Don't restrict her guests (unless one of them appears to have moved in, which you may define as staying overnight without your permission for more than two nights in a row).

Your Live-in Agreement may specify what conveniences you will provide, and at the same time protect you by identifying those items as belonging to you. You may want to let her have use of any or all of the following:

- telephone (with separate number)
- answering machine
- television (with cable connection)/VCR
- CD/tape player
- microwave
- small refrigerator
- coffeemaker
- hot plate or other in-room cooking appliances

If you are the type who likes to deal with all possible annoyances ahead of time, then go ahead and spell out in your Live-in Agreement any conditions that you may want to impose about use of certain items, services, or fixtures. A few examples:

Nanny is responsible for all long distances charges.
Nanny must pay for her own video rentals.
Stereo volume must be kept low after 10 P.M.

Don't go overboard with rules and regulations, but do cover everything usually expected of tenants by landlords, that is: require her to use her space in a way that is legal, and to assume responsibility for acts of negligence or abuse of your property. Make sure she reports to you promptly any problem requiring repair, such as leaky plumbing, signs of pest infestation, and so forth, so that you can take necessary corrective measures before it's too late.

What you should leave out of the Live-in Agreement: Don't try to control her private life, either what she does when she's in her room

Always keep in mind that she is not your daughter, and if she needs supervision like a daughter, then she is not mature enough to be a nanny.

or when she's out of your house. If you are uncomfortable with the idea that she may be doing things under your roof that violate your personal religious or moral values, you probably should not be offering a live-in situation. The same caution applies for parents who are hyper-sensitive to noise.

Procedures During the First Two Weeks

The Orientation Tour

First day. Either you or your spouse should stay home on the nanny's first full day. (It is amazing to me how many parents will invest $1,800 in an agency's fee, followed by another $350 for videotaping, but they won't invest eight hours of their own time to see that things are getting off to a good, safe start!)

Your first order of business should be to give the nanny a thorough orientation tour of your house. The plan for this tour is basically the same as the one described in Chapter Four (the section titled "Stage Two: The House Walk-Through"). While a sharp, attentive nanny will have retained much of the information she learned during that tour, even the most observant will appreciate a second go-round, because this time it's not hypothetical—it's part of the job. This time around, you will spend much more time on specifics. For example, on the interview walk-through, you just pointed out the location of the laundry machines. Now you give a complete lesson in how your child's laundry is to be washed, dried, folded, and put away.

The first-day orientation may go beyond your house and yard, if you like. Familiarize the nanny with your immediate neighbors, and any others who play a regular role in the doings of your household. If you know any other nannies and your children play with the children in their care, be sure they get a chance to meet early on. Get your nanny into "the Nanny Network." This offers many advantages:

- She'll make friends, and start to fit comfortably into your child's world.
- You won't have to worry that she might be too isolated during the day.
- There will be others who see her often, who can give you an outsider's view of how she's getting on.
- Your child will have more opportunity to play with other children.
- If she should have to leave at some later date, the other nannies may be able to help you find her replacement.

Familiarize your nanny with the layout of her new surroundings. Whether she'll be strolling with your baby in a carriage or traveling mostly by car, make sure she has a sense of where the important things are, where the fun things are, where the nearest fire station is, the police station, the nearest emergency room, and so forth. Be sure she knows the way to the children's schools, playground, friends' houses, stores, places to eat, doctor's offices—anywhere your child is likely to go. Be sure she knows your street address and can give others accurate directions to find your house. (This is essential, in case she ever needs to call for an ambulance.)

You don't have to accomplish all these things on the very first day—but try to make sure she's got a good handle on the house, kids' schedules, and neighborhood features by the end of her first week, at the latest.

Spot-checking

The first two weeks with any new nanny you should keep your own work schedule as flexible as possible—and ideally, so should your spouse. You will be making some very important spot-checks for safety's sake. Here's what you do.

Second day. Leave the house for work according to your normal schedule. Hug and kiss the kids, say good-bye to the nanny, and head off toward the bus or subway stop, or get in your car as if you're on your way to work as usual. Five to ten minutes later turn around and head back home. Quietly as possibly, reenter your house, listening as you go for sounds of the nanny and the children. Is everything okay? If so, calmly announce that you left something important behind. (It's the truth, because just prior to leaving, you carefully placed your brief-case in the front hall closet.) Retrieve your briefcase, kiss your kids again, and take your second leave. Without a doubt, that second good-bye will make for a rougher transition for your kid(s)—but it will be worth the trouble to have this brief view of how the nanny is settling in on her second day of work.

Suppose you return home to the sounds of crying or wailing. Keep in mind that it's normal for a child under six to have stranger anxiety and to fuss for a while upon a parent's departure. So don't necessarily hold the commotion against the nanny, but do check to see how she's dealing with the problem. Is she trying to comfort your child? Is she ignoring him/her? Is she angry and upset at being rejected? If it's the middle possibility, keep a sharp eye on how things seem to be prog-ressing over the next several days. There could be trouble ahead. If it's the last choice—fire her on the spot. She just does not have the right temperament for the job.

Later during the same day, you might come home for lunch and/ or come home early in the evening, telling the nanny that you've re-turned to provide a bit more orientation and help to familiarize her with the working environment. Of course, by now she will realize that a key purpose of these visits is to check up on her, but that's all right. Since you've already communicated to her that you are an extremely cautious and involved parent (you said so during her first interview), she will understand that it will take some time for you to develop com-plete trust, and she will be patient with your intrusiveness. If she does become irritated and/or visibly prickly in response to your spot-checks, you will be wise to get rid of her now, before the antagonism has a chance to deepen.

If, after the first three or four of your unexpected appearances, the nanny tries to assure you that your daytime visits are unnecessary, you might want to respond this way (self-deprecating smile optional): "I'm kind of a Nervous Nellie, I guess, when it comes to my baby. I'm sure after we've worked together for a few weeks, I'll settle down, and won't be micromanaging everything the way I've been these first few days."

Sometimes an older nanny will have become too used to ruling the roost to take the parent's spot-checks as anything but interference. As soon as you show up unexpectedly, the nanny will act all huffy and offended, as if you are presumptuous to tell such an experienced professional how you want things done on the job—as if there would ever be a question that she might make a mistake. It is important for you not to let yourself be intimidated by a nanny from the outset, no matter how commanding her presence. If you permit yourself to be put down even once in such a manner, the nanny will cast herself in the role of chief authority over your child's care, and you will automatically fall into the role of second fiddle—and most likely stay there for the remainder of your relationship with that nanny. No matter how many years she's cared for children, remember, you still have seniority when it comes to time spent with your own child. You are still the boss . . . so guard against such early efforts at role reversal.

How many spot-checks should you do altogether? The answer is a function of your own degree of nervousness, the flexibility afforded by your job, and the nanny's own background, demeanor, and references. For example, a nanny with great references from a nearby neighbor might need only one or two spot-checks, because she is very much a known quantity to begin with.

An extremely cautious couple might check in daily during the first week, and then each spouse do one or two spot-checks over the course of the second week. More laid-back types, or those who lack the flexibility to take off in the middle of the workday, may be content to perform only one spot-check on the first workday, one a day or two later, and a third one at some randomly chosen time in the middle of the second week.

You may also recruit friends, neighbors, and other nannies to drop by your house during the first week or two, to get their impressions of how things are going. Make sure the nanny has been introduced to any likely callers ahead of time. As a basic security rule, you do not want your nanny opening your front door to anyone she does not know. The visitor may greet the nanny with the friendly line: "I know you're new in this job, so I just stopped by to see if there was anything I could do to help."

Even if you don't have anyone stop by on purpose to check out your new nanny, you should be sure that your neighbors or their childcare providers are aware that you would welcome their observations. It's all too often assumed that parents must know (and therefore approve) of a nanny's style of supervision—even when she's letting a child run in the street or bite other children. People may shrink from delivering a negative report about a caregiver because they don't want to be viewed as a busybody or tattletale. It's important to let others know, on the contrary, that you value their observations and welcome their comments. Spread the word to all who might be likely to encounter your nanny during the day that you would appreciate hearing anything that would be helpful to you in evaluating her performance. Of course, you should express reciprocal willingness to keep an eye on your neighbor's caregiver whenever you have the chance, as well.

Phoning in. Call often, especially during the first two weeks. It's generally a good idea to call when you expect your child to be napping, so that you won't disrupt any activities. If your child is never asleep when you call within the usual nap time, then you'll want to talk with the nanny about the evident disruption in the child's normal schedule.

If your child isn't a napper, then call randomly, but be sure the nanny knows that taking care of the child takes priority over answering the telephone. If it would be too disruptive for her to pick up (say, for example, during a diaper change or during a bath), she should let your answering machine take the message, and call you back at her convenience.

It's true that the telephone allows a rather limited sense of what's going on at home; on the other hand, there are a few important clues that you should be able to detect: Does the nanny sound calm, and on top of things, more often than not? Or does she sound harried, flustered, even out of breath? How often is your child heard crying in the background? If the answer is "most of the time," you'll want to perform a spot-check—and soon. Is she seldom at home when you expect her to be? If that's the case, consider getting her a cell phone, and call her wherever she may be. Is the TV always on in the background, when you've asked her to limit TV viewing to certain times of the day? Is she able to give you a sense of how the day has gone so far, or is she vague and uncommunicative in response to your questions?

A good, safe nanny will not consider it a burden to speak to the parents regularly over the phone but will welcome the parents' involvement, considering it part of her job to keep the parents fully informed about their child's development.

OPTIONAL: YOUR CHILD'S CARE BOOK

Anne and Jay, both writers, came up with a dynamite idea I'd like to pass along: Make a booklet containing all the important instructions, safety information, and telephone numbers you want your nanny to know. The example the couple showed me was created on their home computer with the aid of an easy-to-learn desktop publishing program. Of course, neat handwriting works just as well.

The booklet opens with a cover page featuring a photograph of their baby over the title: *The Book of Robyn* (the baby's name). Pages have been hole-punched to fit into a three-ring binder. That way, as their child grows and her schedule changes, old information can be deleted, and pages rewritten and reinserted. The whole booklet does not need to be reprinted.

A table of contents gives the nanny a fast way to look up any specific fact. Tab dividers mark off the beginnings of the different sections, including: Important Phone Numbers; Robyn's Routine; Meal Preparation; All About Bedtime; Places to Go; and House Information. If, for example the nanny should notice that a pipe is leaking, all she needs to do is to flip open *The Book of Robyn* to the House Information tab to find the section telling the location of the main water cut-off.

If one day she finds herself running short of ideas for activities, she can open the booklet to Places to Go to find out what outings Robyn has enjoyed in the past. Earlier nannies had some input in compiling the list.

Since Robyn is notoriously difficult to put to bed at night, the section called All About Bedtime is especially useful. It details the expected ritual, suggests time or frequency limits for several of its components (for example, no more than fifteen minutes of story-telling and only one drink of water before the light goes out).

Once you have such a booklet, orientation of each new nanny becomes fast and simple. You just hand her a copy and ask her to study it well before the first day of work.

Video Surveillance

You've seen the ads for rental of hidden video cameras. Maybe you've even seen a segment on your local news, showing a case of child abuse caught on videotape, resulting in a nanny's arrest. You may think to yourself, "That's the way to go. That way I'll be *sure* I've got a safe nanny!"

Before you call for installation or write anyone a big check, consider this: What are you *doing* leaving your child alone in the house with someone you think *for a minute* could be capable of the sort of abuse you've seen on tape? In other words: If you believe there's a very real chance that you'll catch something bad on the videotape, you've *already* got a bad nanny. If she inspires so little confidence, then fire her without delay.

If you haven't yet hired, my advice is as follows: Go through all the steps outlined in Chapter Four about interviewing and reference checking; follow all the suggestions in the section above about spot-checking; and if she passes all these tests with flying colors, relax—you've got a good one—and you don't need to tape her on the sly. If, on the other hand, after all your background checking and reference gathering, you still find yourself with a feeling of unease, you might want to take a look at your own life: Maybe you are just unhappy at the idea of letting anyone else taking care of your baby, while you are stuck at work. If that's the case, then probably no nanny can truly give you peace of mind, however well she performs; you and your spouse might be better off trying to rearrange your lives so that you can be your own nanny and stay at home with your kids.

What if you've done the recommended interviewing and reference checking and nothing questionable has turned up—yet you have no great sense of confidence, either? What if your nanny strikes you as merely the best of a mediocre bunch, and you took her on primarily because you needed to have someone right away? Won't videotaping under those circumstances offer you the reassurance you need?

Not really, and here's why: Your camera is placed in one room, and it is fixed in one position. Suppose you observe nothing wrong on the tape? Why would that give you peace of mind? The nanny could still be abusing your child in another room and you'd never know it.

Consider, too, the fact that the highest risk of injury or death for small children occurs while riding in a car. The hidden camera tells you nothing about whether your nanny always buckles your child properly into the carseat.

Moreover, the parent who relies on hidden cameras instead of on his or her own observations and good judgment may take the absence of abuse on the videotape as proof of the nanny's safety and become complacent. The parent may then conclude it's not necessary to take any of the steps described in the sections above on spot-checking and phone-checking. You want assurance, not just that your nanny is not abusive, but that she is positively influencing your child's development, that she is creative and loving and kind. You want to make sure that your child is forming a bond with her and is happy and thriving under her care. No video camera left running for a few hours at a time is going to tell you those things. To obtain information of that scope requires use of the five human senses—plus a sixth indispensable sense, your parent's intuition (your acute sensitivity to your own child's feelings). If at any point your gut starts sending you a warning: *This feels wrong for my child!*—listen to it, and if necessary, make a change.

ALL-PURPOSE PRINCIPLE FOR NANNY EVALUATION

When it comes to safety, money is never a good substitute for your own sense of the situation—because only you know your child well enough to say with certainty, this nanny is (or is not) a good match for this child.

Firing

Within a few weeks of hiring. Your Employment Agreement should give either side the right to end the relationship for any reason at any time within your designated probationary period. This provision gives you strong incentive to complete your evaluation and come to a definite decision one way or another, about the nanny's future with you, during the allotted time. If you do decide you are unhappy with the nanny's performance, you need not explain, offer a second chance, or try to ease the nanny out gracefully over time. In fact, the less explanation you offer for termination, the easier it will be for the nanny to accept the break (in most cases).

Here are some suggested phrases for delivering the bad news:

"I'm sorry, but it just doesn't seem to be working out."

"We seem to have different approaches to childcare. I think I need someone with more attention to detail" (or "someone who is _____" fill in the blank with any other quality you were disappointed to discover that your nanny lacked).

If you don't like playing the bad guy, you can always shift the blame to your unsuspecting child, like this: "Danielle is so high-strung. I'm sorry, but she just didn't seem to be adjusting to your style of nannying. I'm sure in your next job, with a different, more easygoing child, things will be fine."

Or you can try the "this-is-in-your-own-best-interest" approach: "I get the feeling you're not really happy in this job. I've felt a lot of tension since you've been working, and it seems to me this is probably not the sort of arrangement that suits you best. I'm sure you'll be a lot happier with a different sort of family."

No matter whom you designate as the one to blame, be sure to express your sorrow (sincere, if possible) that things didn't work out as each of you had hoped. Apologies always help to soothe hurt feelings. Make clear, too, that you will give the nanny a good reference for her next job (that is, unless you fired her for some specific, dangerous act). Your reference need not be a rave, just a report limited to those aspects of nanny care that you think she did do well.

Firing beyond the probationary period. By now you have had a fair chance to have decided whether the nanny is meeting your family's needs. By now your children have probably bonded with the nanny, and so her departure will undoubtedly cause them pain. By now the nanny has presumably won your trust and shown that she is basically a decent person, caring and desirous of doing a good job. For these reasons you should only fire if you have no other reasonable alternative.

If, at this point in your relationship, you discover that she has made a mistake in judgment while caring for your children—even a relatively serious mistake—you should figure that she can learn from her error, and give her a second chance.

Of course, there are some mistakes that are just too serious to be forgiven. They indicate, not that the nanny had a one-time lapse in judgment, but that you were wrong about her basic good judgment from the start, and she is not, and never was, worthy of your trust. It is a shame, in such a circumstance, that you did not realize her untrustworthiness during the probationary period, but the minute you do, you need to fire her.

The stories in the box on page 132 are true examples of the sort of mistake a nanny might make and still be kept on.

What kind of mistake would be so serious as to necessitate firing a nanny of long-standing? Offenses that you may consider unforgivable include:

- drunk driving with your children in the car
- leaving your children alone in the house for any length of time
- any act of violence against your child
- violating your specific instructions about childcare after a first warning
- lying to you about a matter pertaining to your child's health or safety

Before you fire, you should have indisputable proof that the offense has occurred. Second-hand reports are to be judged according to the credibility of the source, and the nanny should be given a chance to tell her side of the story.

What happens if you have a suspicion but are not completely sure that a serious breach has occurred? That's a common and unfortunate situation. You might need to undertake some careful sleuthing to determine the truth. Let's take an example: You suspect your nanny has been sneaking drinks from your liquor cabinet while you're at work. First, you must rule out all other suspects. Determine whether your cleaning lady, your daughter's piano teacher, or your teenage stepson also could have gained access to the liquor cabinet during the time in question. Once you've satisfied yourself that you are down to only one possibility, make sure that the liquor is in fact disappearing. An old but effective trick is to secretly mark the level on the bottles on the shelf.

SECOND CHANCES FOR MOLLY AND KIM

Molly asked to borrow the car one evening, and we said okay. She's always been a responsible driver, so we weren't worried. Even when we heard about the accident, at first we thought, "Not a big deal. At least no one was hurt—though the car was totaled." Then it turned out that Molly hadn't been the driver. She'd been out with her boyfriend, they'd both had a few drinks, and she'd let him do the driving. Turns out whenever they went out to-gether, she'd always let him drive. Of course, we were shocked and upset—and for a while we weren't sure whether we were going to keep her on, but then we saw how sorry she was, and we felt very sure she'd never make the same sort of mistake twice, so we accepted her apology and moved on. She worked for us another full year . . . and there were no other incidents, so it turned out we made a very good call.

—Eleanor from Maryland

Kim had worked for us for eight months and our daughter really took to her very well. Kim often did errands for us, picking up dry cleaning, things like that. One day a neighbor told me that she'd seen Kim get out of the car and run into a store, while our daughter was left in her carseat in the back, doors unlocked and the engine running. Kim came back in a minute or two with a package, then got in the car and drove away. When I asked Kim about the inci-dent, she acknowledged that it had happened, but added, "I was only gone for a minute, and I kept the air on, so the baby wouldn't get too hot." Apparently, she never heard of someone driving off in a car with the engine left running. I told her about a story I'd heard on the news, about a car thief who took off in stolen car with a baby in the back, and when he noticed the baby, he threw her, carseat and all, out of the moving vehicle. Well, as soon as Kim heard that story, she understood what a tragedy could have occurred. I believe her when she says she would never do such a thing again. And she believes me when I say it had better not!

—Terry from Virigina

One caution for those tempted to enlist a child as an informant: *Don't!* Your child should never be put in such an emotionally precarious position. Listen carefully and respectfully, however, if a child comes to you of his or her own accord with a credible-sounding account of the nanny's misconduct. These are some questions to help you decide how to evaluate the child's account:

Is your child seven or older? Seven has long been held to be the "age of reason," the time at which a child learns to distinguish between fantasy and reality.

Has your child ever told "tall tales," or enjoyed playing tricks on you in the past? A report from a child with a vivid imagination should be viewed more skeptically than one from a child who has always been literal-minded.

Do the facts of the child's account seem plausible? Are there any wild or improbable elements (such as a monster or a ghost)? You should probably discount the whole story if any part of it is not to be believed.

Avoid the temptation to start asking the child a lot of questions. Be aware that psychological studies have shown consistently that young children will give the answer they think a parent wants to hear. Once you have planted the notion in a small child's mind that you would be interested in stories about bad things the nanny has done, it may be just too tempting for the child to come up with a story, complete with frightening details.

What is a parent to do in such a situation? The nanny has passed through all the checks and screenings and has presumably become a trusted member of the household. And yet you don't want to ignore a possibility that you may have been wrong about her all along.

The fairest, but safest course of action, I would suggest, is to resume spotchecking her during her working hours, at random intervals. Don't go to her with any vague or insubstantial suspicions, but allow her sufficient time under your secretly stepped-up vigilance, to work her way back to a position of full confidence. In all probability, your faith in her will be restored, with no lasting damage done to your relationship.

✴ CHAPTER SIX ✴

TOWARD A LONG-TERM
RELATIONSHIP

Show Respect for the Job She Does

*E*mployers who have lost their nannies to other families sometimes react with bafflement and dismay. "How could she have left us?" they wail. "We treated her just like one of the family!" And it's true, they did—and just like one of their children, they expected her to do chores without extra pay; they put her under a curfew on weeknights; they had rules about taking snacks from the refrigerator and when the TV could be on. They snapped at her when she did not do a task exactly when or how it was supposed to be done; they complained about her friends; they meddled in her private life.

After hearing many such tales from nannies I am drawn to this inescapable conclusion: If you want to build a solid, long-term relationship with your nanny, *don't* treat her as a member of your family—and *especially* not as a child in your family. Treat her as a valued employee and a mature and independent adult, which is exactly what she is (or should be, given the responsibilities of her position).

You may have hired or supervised other adults in your working life before. Try to conduct yourself with the nanny much the same way as you did with those other subordinates. Give them the training and direction they need to fulfill the functions of the job; give them as much initial supervision as is necessary to be sure that they're up to the task; allow them a certain amount of time to earn your full confi-

134

dence—*then leave them alone.* Don't micromanage their days or try to run their social lives.

If you have never hired or supervised anyone in your job before, then turn the situation around: Consider how you, as an employee, prefer to be treated, and treat your nanny accordingly.

Let your nanny put her own creativity to use to think up activities, arrange outings, plan meals, and so forth. Encourage her to read books about children's growth and psychology. Lend her any books of your own that you have found particularly insightful.

Support her efforts to broaden her horizons. If she expresses an interest in pursuing a long-term career goal (especially if it's in a child-related field, such as teaching or children's healthcare), try to accommodate her class schedule as much as you can. You might even offer her some tuition assistance in the form of a bonus or a low-interest loan. (At this point you may be asking yourself, "What is this author saying? Why on earth would I want to do anything that will encourage my nanny to switch careers and leave me?") You do it because:

1. Your help will be much appreciated, and she will return your generosity in the form of extra devotion to your children's care.
2. If you don't help her, she will probably feel frustrated and unhappy, and sooner or later will decide to move on to something else, anyway; and
3. It's the right thing to do.

Let her know you realize that nannying is not one of those jobs that "just anyone" can do well. Parents often make the mistake of thinking, because the job is for a relatively low wage and does not require an advanced degree, that it's an easy job, one that lots of people are qualified to do. Therefore, they don't try to hang on to a good nanny when they find one; they figure nannies are more or less interchangeable, and if one leaves, she can easily be replaced. This attitude can lead very quickly to all kinds of problems. The nanny may get the sense that she's being taken for granted, and she may become resentful and may even quit. The parents may go ahead and replace her without much effort—but this book has been full of warnings about the risks of the fast and cheap approach. There is some truth to the old cliché, you get what you pay for.

The main way to show proper respect, both for the position itself and for the individual chosen to perform the job, is to reward good work with good pay. Start out on the right foot by offering a decent wage, on a par with the pay of other, experienced, full-time professional nannies in your neighborhood. (If that level is above your means, don't stretch, but seek a more affordable alternative, such as a shared nanny or a family day-care situation.) Then, after a year's good work, give your nanny a raise. A year later, be sure to raise again.

Show your appreciation with more than the annual raise. Make sure you remember her birthday (and keep in mind that for someone on a limited budget, the most welcome present is usually cash). Your children, of course, should make their own cards and perhaps a hand-crafted gift, if they are old enough to do so. The same advice goes for Christmas or whatever winter holiday she celebrates. At any time of the year a handwritten note from you and/or your child will mean a lot.

Above all, let her do her job without undue interference. In particular, be careful not to undercut her authority in front of your children. Many of the nannies I interviewed described an occurrence something like the following: The nanny has just said no to a child's request, only to have the parent step in and allow the child to have his or her way. See the boxed story on page 137 for an example.

Of course, you must be sure that your views and the nanny's views about discipline and proper behavior are more or less in sync. This was an area you should have explored thoroughly with her during the interview process and within her probationary work period. It would be most unfortunate, several months into her employment, to discover that your discipline styles are hopelessly at odds. Once you are sure that she understands the disciplinary techniques that you want her to use and you have confidence that she knows what sort of behavior you want to encourage or discourage, you should be able to leave the day-to-day enforcement of rules largely up to her. Giving her such freedom does not set her up as your competitor as an authority figure, but as your lieutenant. You are still the general.

(If you find it hard to allow your nanny enough independence to chart her own course with your children, you may have symptoms of nanny jealousy. See the section on page 145 of this chapter for further discussion of this problem).

"NO RESPECT"
(LAUREN'S STORY)

I used to sit for two little girls: One was six and the other was four. They fought with each other a lot and I was trying to teach them to get along better. The problem was the parents—they frequently made things worse by intervening when I was trying to restore some peace. There was one time the girls were fighting over a doll. The older one had snatched it away from the younger one, and the younger one was screaming about it. I had asked the older girl to hand it back and apologize. Then I wanted the younger one to accept the apology, and after some time with the doll, let her older sister have a turn. Well, the dad heard the ruckus and came in, dried the older one's tears, and when she told him she was crying over the doll, immediately promised her that he would go to the store and buy her an identical one. That was typical—I could never enforce any rules or manners when the parents were home, especially with the older one, who I thought should have known better.

My second big complaint about that job was that the parents never asked me about my plans for the day when the children wanted to do something. I would make an appointment to take a child to get her hair cut. The child asks me if we could stop to get an ice cream first, and I say, no, there isn't time—we'll get one afterward. Then the child goes running to her mom and asks to go to the ice cream store first, and the mom says, "fine." That puts me in a difficult position. The parents were usually careful not to contradict each other's decisions. I would like to be able to count on the same respect. Otherwise, the kids quickly learn they can go around me to get whatever they want, and they don't have to take what I say very seriously.

I was glad when that job ended.

Communicate Effectively

Many parents create a regular channel of communication with the nanny to use as part of their daily routine. They may set aside a particular time slot each day (usually at the end of the workday) for the nanny and one or both parents to sit down together and talk, just to make sure anything important (or even anything unimportant, but interesting, helpful, or funny) gets discussed. Regular talks establish a sense of two-way openness, so that the nanny feels it's normal to go to the parents as soon as she notices a problem, however small; the parents feel it's normal to go to the nanny with anything about her management of the house or oversight of their children that worries them. This way each side has a pressure release: There is little danger that a problem will keep simmering until one day it suddenly explodes in everyone's face.

A few parents go farther than just talking about things as they go along; they ask the nanny to keep a daily log or journal of what goes on during the day. For some nannies (especially those minding two or more children), this daily requirement will be a burden, a distraction from the many other duties that need to be accomplished each day. On the other hand, there are those nannies who welcome the chance each day to reflect, evaluate, and then write up their observations. It's an individual matter for parents to consider and discuss with the nanny as they set up her work schedule.

In the other direction, there are many parents who prefer not to formalize communication through time set-asides or report writing. They just make sure they can chat easily with the nanny on any subject, and that they have the sense that the nanny feels comfortable coming to them, keeping them informed about their child's day. They talk with the nanny over the phone quite a bit during the work week, but there is no regular pattern or areas of coverage to their conversations. This informal method of communication can serve just as well, if it suits both the parents' and the nanny's personal style.

The problem comes when parents don't take any time to think about avenues of communication. They may be so busy at work that they don't call in; and the nanny is too timid or too unsure of herself to flag the parents' attention when something is starting to go awry.

Then one day the situation worsens, a crisis occurs, and the parents are left wondering, "How could this have happened?"

If you want to make sure you are never caught thinking the same, just follow these few simple rules:

- From day one, pick a regular mode of communication (daily log, daily sit-down chat, or frequent phone calls) and make sure you use it.
- Always take your nanny's calls. Don't let your secretary tell your nanny "you're in a meeting," when you're not.
- When you first get the impression that something is bothering your nanny, find out what it is. Don't let things slide.
- When something is bothering you, come out with it. Be tactful, but at the same time, make your point.
- Don't lecture or scold. Always address her with respect, speaking as you would to anyone in a position of responsibility and trust.

And remember, there are few problems that can't be solved when people of goodwill, who care about the same things, put their heads together.

Build a Friendship

There is nothing that says that a boss and a subordinate can't be friends. It happens in the workplace all the time. Many parents, however, are afraid to let a friendship develop—some thinking that the nanny will take advantage, others assuming that they will end up losing their authority in the process. There is, one must concede, a certain inescapable awkwardness about the prospect. After all, you don't pay your other friends . . . and you can't fire them either.

If the whole idea strikes you as an iffy proposition, then don't feel you have to try; keep some degree of formality in your relationship, rather than force a feeling of intimacy that's not sincere.

If, on the other hand, you've been able to make friends both up and down the hierarchical ladder at your job, then you will probably be able to do so with an employee at home as well. The key is to follow your own feelings, and not act any differently than you would with any other new person in your social life. If you find her company pleasant, and can talk to her easily, then you have a good basis to expand your contacts beyond the bounds of the typical employer-employee relationship.

Most employers will find they have at least two important interests in common with their nannies: the love of the children in the household, and the desire to see them kept happy and safe. As with any friendship, if you will treasure it, nurture it, and also give it some time, it will grow and give back to you in many rewarding ways.

As you would with any friend, you can show an interest in her personal life—but thoughtfully, considerately, and without turning into a busybody.

Caution: Proceed in this direction only if you are prepared to be nonjudgmental about her lifestyle choices. See the section titled "Party Girls" on page 149 of this chapter for further discussion on this point.

Talk to her about non-work-related subjects as you would to any friend: You can discuss movies, books, fashion, or the news of the day—but be sure not to let any arguments get started if you discover that you don't always see things the same way. If you find yourself wanting to spend more time with her, then consider getting another babysitter to come in some night, while you and your spouse take her out to dinner. You might want to let her bring along a guest (especially if she has a steady boyfriend).

By cultivating her friendship you gain more than just the pleasure of her company beyond the workday. You may also win her personal confidence. As your friend, she will probably let you in on her thoughts, plans, and dreams, long before she takes any action that could affect her employment in your house. You'll be among the first to find out, for example, that she's fallen in love and is thinking about moving out of state with her boyfriend.

Be sure to note the box below. Let me end this section with a story

---

DON'T OVERSTEP THE BOUNDS OF FRIENDSHIP

⏰ You don't want her to start wondering if your interest in her personal life might be motivated mainly by a desire, as an employer, to keep yourself in the know. So when she comes to you with her problems, try your best to react as a friend *and only a friend.* You are probably older, and arguably wiser, but that doesn't mean she wants you to tell her what to do. When she wants a mother's advice, she probably knows where she can go to get it.

---

illustrating what can happen if you fail to respect the normal boundaries of friendship, and start to meddle in the nanny's personal life. Let us suppose that your nanny has lately been complaining to you about her boyfriend's lack of consideration. Reacting mainly as a mother, not as a friend, you say: "Dump him!" You tell her he's bad news, and you say you've known it all along. Now let's say she follows your advice. Here's what happens next: A week later she finds herself feeling miserable and full of longing, and she blames *you.* When she finally makes up her mind to get back together with the boyfriend, she does so knowing how much you disapprove. If she's the sensitive type, she'll feel torn, and may want to extract herself from the situation that now seems to her to be fraught with conflict. Rather than give up the boyfriend, she'll give up the job. Remember, if a friendship founders over bad advice, you may be able to patch it up in time—but it's hard to get back a good nanny who quits in a huff.

Better Living with a Live-in

Have you ever had a roommate? Did you get along? Oftentimes the unpleasant memories of shared dorm rooms and difficult apartment-mates fade away long before you're settled with kids and ready to hire live-in help. That goes a long way toward explaining why parents are nearly always caught off-guard by the conflicts that typically arise from the live-in nanny situation.

Your first step, then, before you advertise for a live-in employee, should be to step back and think critically about yourself and your house habits. Are you basically a laid-back kind of person, able to get along and go along with almost anything? If so, keep on reading. If not, stop now, before you start doing anything that may be hard to reverse. Live-in is probably not going to be for you.

Next, think about the kind of accommodations you could provide. Is the space nice enough to attract someone with high standards? ("Just okay" will probably only get you a "just okay" sort of live-in.)

What should a live-in situation have to attract a good nanny? Many parents with long-term relationships with good live-ins gave me plenty of tips and suggestions in response to this question. The list below is compiled from my interview notes. To maximize comfort and minimize the potential for conflict, your live-in situation should provide:

Telephone. Put in a separate telephone line and answering machine for the nanny's exclusive use. Otherwise you will likely be in regular conflict with the nanny about how much of her free time she spends on the phone. With her own line you will have no trouble figuring out which were her long-distance calls. Of course, you should pay for the installation charges and for the local monthly service.

Adequate privacy. A room with its own separate entrance is ideal. If you are trying to decide which part of your house to make over into the nanny's room, go with the one that provides such access. That is, given a choice between finishing off an attic room or finishing off one in the basement, choose the basement, so that the nanny can enter and exit through the basement door. Even if you must spend some extra money for carpeting, improved lighting, or installation of baseboard heat, you will be glad you did. A separate entrance gives her something of the sense of having a private apartment. *Never* force a nanny to share a room with a child, or use a portion of a larger room, such as the family room or the children's playroom.

Bathroom. Some high-end nanny agencies will not even place a nanny in a live-in situation that requires her to share a bathroom with anyone else in the house. But providing a separate bathroom does more than help you attract a choosy nanny; it makes your life less stressful once you've got her. No waiting in line at the door, no danger that your curious little boy will barge in on her in the tub; no anxiety that she's used the wrong toothbrush or finished off your favorite shampoo. If you don't have a spare bathroom to dedicate to her use, call a bathroom contractor and find out how quickly one can be added. You might be surprised at how cheap and easy it is to install a prefab shower, a small sink, and toilet in an existing large closet or tucked away under a staircase.

Cooking facilities. Give her the ability to cook for herself, apart from the family. Your live-in space doesn't need to include its own kitchen—though that would, of course, be nice. But any room with a bookshelf can support a small microwave, and if you've got the power capacity at the outlets, you can add a hotplate, a coffeemaker, and a mini-fridge. Do insist that any food be stored safely, and any mess promptly tidied up, so that your house will remain free of roaches and other pests. You must also be sure she's not the absent-minded type who would forget to turn off any cooking appliance when leaving the house. If you are not confident of her attention to detail when it comes to kitchen safety, you certainly should not be hiring her as your nanny.

Entertainment. Why should anyone have to fight with their nanny over what TV shows to watch, what movies to rent, what music to listen to? A TV, VCR, and CD player should not set you back an inordinate amount, especially if you shop the yard sales. The only substantial sums you may need to lay out will come in the form of sound-proofing for a house with thin walls. You may want to replace hollow-core doors with solid wood ones, blow in foam insulation (which will, at the same time, make a cold basement room feel warm and snug), hang noise-absorbing curtains on the windows, and/or install quilted, sound-absorbing wallpaper.

Hospitality. Let her friends and relatives come to visit. Of course, you're not running a hotel, and so there are limits to how long her mother from Martinique may stay. And you definitely don't want her boyfriend making your house into his permanent rent-free home, either. The place to set out these limits is in your Live-in Agreement, but do try to be generous, or at the very least, reasonable. When she has a relative or a close friend come to stay for a few nights, be gracious and welcoming, as you would be to your spouse's guests. Friends who visit just for a few hours in the evening or on weekends can be viewed strictly as *her* guests, to be entertained in her own live-in space as she likes. (That's yet another reason why it's helpful for your nanny to have a separate entrance, her own cooking facilities, and as much sound-proofing as possible.) Many a nanny has moved out abruptly from a household, not over anything to do with childcare, but because of a conflict over guests.

Clear delineation between working and non-working hours. When your live-in nanny is not working, treat her as if she is not available. It's tempting, when you wake up on Saturday morning to find your children running wild all over the house, to greet the nanny as she emerges from her room with a plea for help. Resist this urge with all your might. A live-in's time off means as much to her as it does to a live-out—only she's seldom in a position to insist upon it. Parents can all too easily take advantage of her constant proximity to get constant work out of her—free of charge. But there's no word for this situation other than exploitation—even if she's too timid to complain. What sometimes happens is that the nanny goes on "helping out" without objecting, but all the while feeling it's unfair. As time goes on the feeling just keeps growing, until she reaches the snapping point. Then the day comes that you really, really need her to mind the kids an hour early for you—and you knock on her door, but she's gone. Without so much as a word to anyone, she has cleared out and taken off into the night, because she was too scared to stand up for her rights face to face. (Don't let this become your story.)

Sense of belonging. Let her make the place her own. Just giving her a bed and a cast-off dresser isn't enough. If you want her to be with you for the long haul, you've got to give her a sense that it's her home, too. Let her exercise her personal decorating tastes: Let her repaint (if she's lived there six months or longer.) Let her hang her pictures. If you're replacing the carpeting or choosing new curtains, let her pick them out (within certain budgetary limits, of course). You trust her enough to look after your child; surely you can trust her to pick a color scheme (and if it turns out to be a little too much for your personal tastes, look at this way—at least you'll be prepared for the day your teenager is ready to make a similar choice!)

Watch Out for the Little Green Monster! (Jealousy)

There are three distinct types of mother/nanny jealousy:

Type One is **jealousy over time.** The mother sees the nanny spending all day, every working day, with the children, doing fun things the mother would like to do herself, and the mother becomes jealous.

Type Two is **jealousy over the child's affection.** The mother hears her child say "I love you" to the nanny, or sees her child cuddling with the nanny, and she worries that the child might love the nanny best.

Type Three is **jealousy over the husband.** The mother worries—justly or unjustly—that her husband may be attracted to the nanny, or worse, may be acting on that attraction.

All three types of jealousy, if not quickly addressed, can cause serious problems, and even spell disaster for the family.

Type One jealousy is perhaps the most normal and widespread. We love our kids and so we want to be with them more. A good nanny *does* appear to be having fun, much of the time. The key question to ask yourself is, "How often do you feel this way?" If it's an occasional thought once or twice a day when you talk on the phone to the nanny, then don't worry about it further. If you are still basically satisfied with your job, then stop and remember what it was that led you to choose your career path, and be happy that have found a good nanny who can allow you to enjoy both motherhood and your career at the same time.

The only time you need to be concerned is if you find yourself absorbed in jealous thoughts, not just from time to time, but most of the time. Not only that, but your jealousy has also made you unhappy in your work, or unhappy when you're home. You may find yourself being too critical of the nanny or acting out your negative emotions toward her in any number of other ways. If that's the case, the only sure cure is for you to stop doing what you no longer love and start doing what you really want to do—stay home. Some jobs permit you to take a sabbatical for a period of time. Other jobs can be done from home (either full- or part-time). Be creative, but not impulsive. You will need to give at least as much time and consideration to such a change as you did to hiring a nanny in the first place.

Type Two jealousy is also normal and commonplace. What mother isn't hurt to see her toddler greet her at the end of a long, hard workday, not with "Mommy, you're home!" but with a crying, begging plea to the nanny, "Don't leave! Don't leave!" Yet it can happen to even the most affectionate of mothers. Still, you've got to keep such scenes in perspective. When expressing their emotions, small children may be intense, unpredictable, and obsessive. Their actions may not be well correlated to the deeper meaning of the bonds they've formed with those they love. Be assured no matter what your child may say or do, you will always occupy an unchallengeable position of love. It's just that there's room in his or her heart for others, too. You can be grateful that you were able to find someone who could win your child's devotion. Loving someone and being loved back ultimately helps children, as they mature, to express their own strong feelings for others. You just need to be patient. Remember, too, that you were the one to provide this nanny. Their love for her is inextricably bound up in their love for you.

Type Three jealousy is the most dangerous one, especially if the marriage has already become strained due to the changes and stresses that accompany new parenthood. What action you take depends on whether your jealousy is baseless or grounded in reality. If the nanny is young and pretty and you just can't help thinking your husband wants her, that's not *her* fault. If your husband really has not been flirting, then it's not his fault either. Your self-confidence in that case needs a boost, and you might benefit from talking out your unsubstantiated fears with a therapist—and *only* your therapist. You don't want to let anything slip out that could harm your relationship with either the nanny or your spouse. Recommended action: Just sit tight and try to work through your negative emotions (with professional help, if you so choose), for everyone's sake.

Now let's turn to the second of the Type Three jealousy situations, in which your husband really *is* interested in the nanny—but she's not the husband-snatching type. Here your choice is clear: Between a good, devoted nanny and a cad of a husband, which one do you keep? I say stick with the nanny. Straying husbands are a dime a dozen, but a good nanny is a treasure.

In the third of the Type Three jealousy situations, the husband and the nanny really are hot for each other, and it's not your imagination. Watch out for what I call the Robin Williams maneuver: He separates from you, and after a decent interval, he marries your ex-

---

AVOID THIS JEALOUSY-BORN ERROR!

While you're waiting out the "nanny comes first" phase of your child's development, it's important not to compete with the nanny. Especially avoid the mistake of trying to bribe yourself back into the number one spot with your child by means of toys or treats. Not only will such actions put the nanny at an unfair disadvantage, but you will also spoil your child, and lead him or her to think that love can and should be measured in material things.

---

nanny. Recommended action: Wish I had something to say on this score! Once you've made two critical early errors (choosing a lemon for a husband, then compounding the error by picking a sexual predator for a nanny), I'm afraid there's no way out. Your best bet is prevention: During the interview process keep your antennae tuned for electricity flying between the two. If he's looking at her and she's looking at him with more interest than either of them is showing toward the kids, say: "Next!"

A final thought about mother/nanny jealousy: If you're prone to the emotion, stick strictly with live-out. You don't need to have to deal with the issue in your home twenty-four hours a day. Separation of the nanny's day into work time and free time away from your family will, in that case, be as much a benefit for you as it will be for her.

Servant Culture Nannies

Sometimes it happens that a family is unable to develop close ties with their nanny because of a perception on the nanny's part that she mustn't rise "above her place." Such an attitude is more common among nannies who come from third world countries, where there is, generally speaking, a great social as well as economic divide between employers and workers. I call those nannies who regard their employers as their masters "servant culture nannies," because they view themselves as servants, not childcare professionals.

A servant culture nanny may be devoted to her charges' care; she may be mature and responsible; she may be someone you would trust with your life—and yet you would never call her your friend. No matter how many times you tell her you prefer to be called by your first name, she will still call you "Mrs.," or "ma'am." You may give her full authority to arrange play dates and outings for your children, yet she will still call for your approval of her every plan. None of that may make much of a difference early on, but what really does worry you is what may happen as your child grows up. The nanny may begin to defer to the child, to treat him (or her) as her master, too. She will allow him to be rude to her, to issue orders to her without so much as a please or a thank you, and she will never say no to him.

This "master child, servant nanny" syndrome is something I have seen frequently, and it is cause for alarm. The obvious cure appears to be not to hire someone who is overly deferential, or who comes into the interview acting like an inferior. But to take that approach would be to pass over many otherwise excellent nannies in the hiring process.

A more practical approach is to help the nanny redefine herself at a higher level in her own estimation. If she thinks of herself as uneducated, lacking specialized skills, allow her to acquire some formal qualifications that would increase her standing in her own eyes, and in the eyes of the larger community. Sign her up for evening classes at your local community college or adult education center. She may benefit from formal training in first aid, baby and childcare, or other childrelated courses, or simply study to be able to earn her high school equivalency diploma or even a college degree.

At the same time that you are encouraging her to stop viewing her role as that of a low-level worker, try to prevent her from casting you in the role of the master. Make it a point in all your business dealings with her to treat her not as a servant but as a valued employee. Above all, make sure that your child knows the nanny must be treated with respect, and that she is the main authority figure of the house when Mom and Dad aren't there.

If, after these efforts, your nanny still strikes you as too subservient, you might switch to a different approach. Appeal to her culture's strong sense of family. Rather than try to make her view herself as a professional, try putting her in the role of an honorary auntie or other respected relation. You might even want your child to call her Auntie So-and-So.

With patience and understanding on your part, and with the nanny's own devotion and goodwill toward your family, you should be able to build up a strong, healthy relationship that will be of service to you both.

Party Girls

A common problem with many nannies (and a complaint I have heard particularly from parents who have employed nannies from the wealthier nations of western Europe) is not that they're too timid and subservient (as discussed above), but that they're not as quiet and demure as the parents had expected they would be. These nannies like to stay out late, go to clubs and parties, and their sex lives are more, well . . . adventurous than the parents are prepared to put up with. The box on pages 150–151 contains some typical parents' complaints.

Here are a couple of suggestions for dealing with a hard-partying nanny:

Compartmentalize your complaints: Strictly separate out all those problems that stem from her live-in status from those that stem from her childcare performance. Problems caused by her lifestyle can often be resolved by increasing the degree of residential separateness: installing a separate telephone line for her, sound-proofing her room, arranging for her to use a separate entrance—whatever you can do to make it seem as if she has her own separate apartment in your house. Once you have done that, let her conduct life after hours as she sees fit. An alternative (and perhaps simpler) solution is to arrange for her to live out.

If her fast lifestyle is spilling over into her performance as a nanny, that's an entirely different story. Consider what she's doing wrong and take immediate and appropriate action. Tell her flatly: "No boyfriends around during working hours." Don't tolerate, even once, drinking or taking drugs on the job. Lateness, or a bleary-eyed, hung-over condition affecting alertness should get perhaps one warning—at most two—and then termination. (If you followed the recommendations in this book about setting a probationary period and doing a lot of checking up during that time, presumably you will have been made aware of her wild lifestyle early on, and you will be able to end the relationship without a lot of hassle. If you have discovered problems after the probationary period is over, then be sure her offenses merit the severity of your response.)

There are, of course, some borderline cases: The nanny is fine at her job, which is mainly looking after your infant, but you still fear that her off-hours behavior sets a bad example for your nine-year-old daughter. That's a judgment call. You may want to try to get her to tone down her appearance, or at least require her to be discreet about her social life when your daughter might overhear.

What if you just are offended personally, by her looks, by her sexualized style of dress, by her promiscuous behavior? Your personal feelings *do* matter when it comes to someone who plays an intimate role in your life. It's no good trying to build up trust in a person when you have an underlying sense of unease and disapproval. It's generally wise to root out any essential differences in lifestyle before the nanny becomes a member of your family circle. However, if it is rather late when you finally conclude that things aren't working out, then handle the termination gently. Try to ease her out by steering her toward another, more compatible household, if you can. That way she'll be happier and you will, too—a win-win situation.

Whatever approach you take, keep in mind that your number one priority is not your personal or philosophical level of comfort but your child's safety and well-being. When you know that's assured, you can consider all other problems to be secondary, and do your best to work them out.

LIFE WITH VERONIKA AND DEIRDRE

We imagined when we arranged to bring a Swedish girl over that we'd be getting a good, strong farm girl, like my Swedish ancestors who emigrated to Wisconsin. We didn't expect anything

like Veronika. When she stepped off the airplane she was wearing a tiny black-leather miniskirt and a halter top. Plus thigh-high boots with stiletto heels. We were uneasy from the start, but we thought everything was going to turn out okay, since she seemed great with the kids. But her personal life! It was wild! Out clubbing every night, home at dawn, and on weekend nights, not home at all. It didn't seem to affect her work—she was always ready to go on time. Still, her high living bothered us—even though the baby was too young for us to worry about the kind of example she was setting. We didn't know how to tell her to cool it, so there was always a certain tension in the house. She sensed our disapproval over her lifestyle. Then one day she just quit. She told us she'd found another job where she'd felt she'd get along better with the parents. We didn't argue . . . it was her decision. Still, it did leave us scrambling for childcare for a few rough weeks.
—Ed and Susan from Falls Church, Virginia

My relationship with Deirdre was rocky from the first. I wanted a good Irish Catholic girl, I suppose. It never occurred to me that someone from Dublin would run around the way she did and have so many boyfriends. After she'd been out sick for three days, we learned that she was recovering from an abortion. I suppose the eyebrow ring and the nose stud should have tipped me off that she wasn't quite the blushing rose she'd seemed to be from her résumé. Well, we clashed with her over this and that—who could call her on the phone and how late they could call, and whether or not she could have a boy stay overnight—until finally one day she took off on the back of some guy's motorcycle, and I never saw her again. My kids still miss her deeply, but I knew it was really for the best. The next time I advertised, I used my church's newsletter and the bulletin board at the church day-care center. Eventually, we found a grandmotherly type from the Dominican Republic, very devout, whose personal values are much closer to my own.
—Donna from Germantown, Maryland

CHAPTER SEVEN

TRAINING THE SAFE NANNY

Safety in All Areas

*M*ost nannies, generally speaking, will be only as focused on safety as their employers expect them to be. It is up to you, first of all, to familiarize yourself with all aspects of childcare safety, and then make sure your nanny is trained to work to the standards you set. As discussed in Chapter Four, you should already have set some basic conditions for hiring. You have made sure that your nanny is either already CPR-certified, or you have made arrangements for her to take a certification course upon hiring.

Now make sure she understands and will observe safety rules in all of the following areas:

In the home, including:

- bath safety
- kitchen safety
- diaper duty
- basement safety
- baby-proofing
- baby equipment
- sleep safety
- toy safety

Out of doors, including:

- garden safety
- sandboxes
- swingsets, slides, and other play structures
- pool safety
- sun sense
- driveway safety
- street safety

On the go, including:

- in the car
- in other vehicles
- emergency road procedures
- on bikes, trikes, ride-ons, skates, and sleds
- on visits and outings

If you followed the recommendations in Chapter Four, you have already raised your main safety concerns during the interview, and you have conducted an extensive walk-through of your home, pointing out your child-proofing efforts in every room as you went along. Your nanny should have been thoroughly impressed before hiring by the high priority you place on safety awareness. (She may have even come to the conclusion that you are a bit of a nut on the subject—and that's okay!)

Your Employment Agreement furthermore has laid out a probationary period during which you will check carefully to see that your safety rules are being observed. By now you have made abundantly clear to the nanny that her job depends on her ability to be safe in all areas.

Safety Around the House

Train your nanny to observe all the safety precautions listed below.

In the bathroom. Make sure your medicine cabinet is latched or locked so that all medicines are inaccessible to a climbing, exploring child. All cleansers should be stored, tightly capped, in cabinets that a toddler cannot open. Many parents keep the toilet latched, as well; others instruct the nanny never to leave a small child in the bathroom unsupervised.

Particular care must be taken during bathing. Bath-water temperature should always be checked by wrist or body part other than the fingertips. A bath thermometer is a handy safety device. Bath mats or tub treads are essential to prevent slips and falls. An inviolable rule is that nanny is *never under any circumstances* to leave a small child unattended in the tub, whether the child is in a protective bath ring or not. Instruct her to let the answering machine pick up calls during bath time, or have her take a portable phone into the bathroom with her.

In the kitchen. Point out the kitchen fire extinguisher to the nanny and brief her on its operation. She should follow common-sense rules, such as not to wear loose, flowing sleeves while cooking, and to keep long hair tied back. She should keep pot handles turned to the side or back of the stove. Recommended safety devices include a burner shield, so that little hands can't reach up and touch the stovetop, and knob covers so that only an adult can turn a burner on.

Go over the rules for safe food handling. The nanny should wash her hands with warm soapy water before she begins to cook; the children should do so before they sit down to eat. She should prepare all baby bottles according to the hygienic method preferred by the parents. Formula or breastmilk not consumed within an hour must not be put back in the refrigerator but must be discarded. Meats are to be cooked until the juices run clear; there should be no pinkness visible on the inside or outside. A meat thermometer may be used for complete assurance that the cooking temperature is high enough to kill all harmful bacteria. Fruits and vegetables must be thoroughly washed before consumption. Particular care should be taken with eggs—not only are they to be cooked until no runny part is left, but raw eggs are never to be used to make any dish that does not call for thorough cooking. That means no eggnog, no hollandaise sauces, and no letting anyone take a lick from a bowl of cake or cookie batter. Honey must never be given to infants one year or younger because of the possible presence of a type of botulism, harmless to older children, that is toxic to an infant's immature stomach.

Always make sure your nanny is aware of any particular food allergies or sensitivities that your children may have. She should be trained

> Here's a simple, essential rule that applies to all leftover foods:
> *When in doubt, throw it out!*

to respond to choking with the Heimlich maneuver (the infant or the child version) and have handy access to the number of a twenty-four-hour poison control hotline. She should know which foods pose a danger of choking to a toddler-sized windpipe and always take precautions, such as slicing grapes in half, and cutting hot dogs into bite-sized pieces, before serving to a child under the age of five.

On diaper duty. Establish a procedure for germ control to be followed with every diaper change, and make sure nanny does not deviate from it. You may wish to put boxes of disposable latex gloves next to every diaper table in the house. Disposable table liners are also a useful convenience, so that you won't have to worry if the table is being properly disinfected after each use.

With every diaper change the nanny should:

- remove the dirty diaper to the appropriate receptacle (the trash can, if you're using disposables; the diaper pail, for cloth).
- clean the baby completely with baby wipes or wet washcloths, taking care not to contaminate the urinary opening with the child's feces. Don't reuse dirty cloths on the child—wipe once and get a fresh cloth for the next wipe.
- dry the child's bottom thoroughly, as any wetness left on the skin will contribute to diaper rash. Avoid powders that the child may breathe in during the process. If rash is present, try a soothing, thick barrier cream such as Desitin or Diaperene.
- put on a new diaper and remove the baby to a secure location (such as the crib or playpen) before attending to clean-up of the changing table. Never leave a baby alone on the table, even if the baby is strapped in with a safety strap. The baby could easily wiggle free.
- dispose of the table liner and/or clean the changing surface with bleach or antibacterial cleaner.

- wash hands before going to retrieve the baby from crib or playpen.

In the basement. By use of door locks, doorknob covers, or childproof latches, restrict access to the utility area, storage closets, deep freezer, and/or basement refrigerator. Children have been known to hide in any accessible, small spaces and become trapped. To prevent scalding, set the thermostat of your whole-house hot-water heater to 120° Fahrenheit or lower. In the laundry area, be careful not to leave detergents or bleach on open shelves, even high ones. Toddlers do like to climb. Small children should not be underfoot when certain laundry tasks are being done. Bleach bottles can suddenly spill, causing burns on contact to baby's sensitive skin, or blinding upon eye contact. Liquid detergents, especially lemon-scented ones that may smell like lemonade, are attractive to toddlers, who may stick in a finger and take a taste before you have a chance to act. The nanny should not be doing any ironing, even if with care, while the children are nearby. See-through baby gates are a good idea, so that the nanny may keep an eye on a toddler in an adjacent playroom, while she attends to the wash.

Baby-proofing. Make sure:

- Unused outlets have outlet covers.
- Any loose wires are tacked down.
- Lamps can't be pulled over, and are also kept away from curtains. Never place a halogen lamp in a baby's room.
- Doors to any areas to be kept inaccessible have locks or doorknob covers.
- Fragile objects have been removed to upper shelves beyond the climbing ability of your exploring child.
- Stairs have gates at the top and bottom.
- Tall, heavy, or bulky pieces of furniture (such as bookshelves or filing cabinets) are secured to the wall by means of a brace or brackets.
- Other safety devices are in place as needed: an edge bumper for a protruding brick hearth; corner covers for coffee tables and other pieces of furniture with sharp corners; and cabinet locks on all cabinets where cleaning supplies, paints, pesticides, lawn care products, or other hazardous chemicals are stored.

- Upper-story windows are kept closed, or are cracked opened only a few inches, or are opened only from the top. Window screens must never be relied upon to restrain a child from falling. (See the boxed story below as a warning.)

Parents who are not confident that they can baby-proof sufficiently on their own may want to hire a service that will go over every inch of their house or apartment for them with safety in mind. Baby-proofing services advertise in local parenting and neighborhood newspapers, and may charge a flat fee based on the size of the house, or may charge by the hour and by the cost of the safety devices installed.

Using baby equipment. For each piece of equipment listed below, take note of the following safety precautions:

For strollers: Make sure your nanny knows how to fold and unfold your stroller safely. Show her how to work the brake and make sure she knows to set it whenever she parks the stroller anywhere. She should be particularly careful about loading packages onto the back of an umbrella-style stroller (they tip over easily).

For port-a-cribs: Serious accidents, and even a few fatalities, have resulted from babies left in port-a-cribs with the side rails not properly locked in place. After set-up the adult should always lean with full weight on each side of the port-a-crib to make sure that the crib will not fold up unexpectedly.

For baby swings (wind-up or battery-operated): The chief danger is overuse. The nanny should be told not to leave the baby in the swing for more than a set amount of time, depending on the circumstances.

LEARN FROM THE ERIC CLAPTON TRAGEDY

In 1991, famed guitarist Eric Clapton was staying on an upper floor of a New York high-rise with his four-year-old son and the boy's mother when a tragic accident occurred. A maintenance man had opened the floor-to-ceiling windows for cleaning, without checking to see if there were any small children in the apartment. The boy fell out and died instantly as he hit the ground.

STROLLER SAFETY: JEAN'S OBSERVATION

Jean was at a shopping mall food court one day with her baby, enjoying lunch, when she noticed a nanny wheeling an umbrella stroller, its handles looped with many shopping bags. As soon as the nanny sat down, taking her hands off the stroller, the weight of all the packages caused the stroller to tip over backward, with the baby strapped inside. Jean said, "You could hear the back of the baby's skull hit the tile floor with a KLUNK!" Every mother in the food court turned her head. The nanny didn't even move for a full three seconds. By then four of five other mothers had dashed over, to pull the stroller upright and see if the baby was okay. Fortunately, he wasn't seriously hurt—though he was screaming at full blast. I thought about going over to ask the nanny the name of her employer. I thought somebody ought to call the parents and tell them how careless their nanny had been—and how unconcerned she seemed by the accident that resulted. But in the end, I suppose I chickened out.

For example, you might say that twenty minutes is long enough for an alert and active baby to be confined in one position, but allow the baby to take a nap of up to one hour in the swing. To check to see that your limits are being observed, make it a point during your daily phone calls to find out exactly where in the house the baby is located at the moment of the call. Make these spot-check calls at varying times during the day for the first two weeks. If the answer to the question, more often than not, is that the baby is in the swing, you probably have a lazy nanny, and may need to make a change.

For baby seats, infant feeding chairs, and bouncer seats: The above rule on time limits is equally applicable. In addition, make sure nanny knows she must always check to be sure the seat is not in danger of falling off the kitchen table, counter, or whatever surface it is on. Babies can jiggle and bounce in their seats, causing some sideways drift. A fall from table or counter height can easily cause a skull fracture or even a fatal brain hemorrhage.

For high chairs: The nanny should know not to leave the baby unattended while she goes to the bathroom or anywhere else. Babies have been known to work their way out of straps, tumbling headfirst to the floor. They can slip down under the seat belts, getting caught by the neck and strangled. They can choke on their food (see the boxed story below). You get the idea—make sure your nanny does, too.

For baby walkers: The American Pediatric Association urges a ban on these products altogether. Baby walkers are a major cause of admissions to emergency rooms nationwide. Still, babies love them and parents, seeing how much their babies enjoy them, are reluctant to give them up. If you do decide to let your baby use a walker, be absolutely certain that there is no way the walker could go down the stairs (that's the number one cause of accidents involving baby walkers). Limit time spent in the walker to twenty minutes, with an adult close at hand the entire time and able to intervene.

For doorway jumpers: Double-check the installation before use, by testing the jumper with a large sack of dog food, or some other heavy object approximately the baby's weight. Pull hard on the jumper, swing

HIGH CHAIR SAFETY
ALICE'S STORY

When I was seven, I was at school one day while my two-year-old brother was home with a babysitter. He was sitting in his high chair, having fried chicken for lunch. It had bones in it, and supposedly my baby brother had always liked to gnaw on them. (I think he was teething.) He was doing that when the doorbell rang. The nanny went to answer it, and when she came back, she noticed he wasn't breathing. He had choked on a chicken bone. This was thirty years ago, so I don't think they had the Heimlich maneuver then. Or maybe they did, but the nanny didn't know how to do it. She called for an ambulance right away, but it was still too late. That's how I lost my baby brother. Believe me when I tell you I would never let anyone walk out of a room with my baby in a high chair.

it back and forth, turn it around, put it through all the motions that a normal, high-energy baby is likely to use. Be sure the jumper will not come into contact with other pieces of furniture and that the baby cannot become entangled in the coils, straps, or ropes. Make sure the nanny knows how to take the baby in and out without excessive tugging. She should observe the twenty-minute maximum as advised for other pieces of equipment.

Sleep safety. You baby's crib should have a firm mattress. To protect the mattress from diaper accidents, lay down a waterproof pad. All other bedding should be made of light, breathable fabrics. Your baby does not need and should not use a pillow. To reduce the danger of sudden infant death syndrome (SIDS), a baby under a year old should always be laid on its back or side, never face down to sleep. If the baby is allowed to sleep in bed with an adult, that adult should not be a deep sleeper (and, especially, should not have consumed alcohol or taken any sleeping aids before going to bed). Keep all pillows and heavy covers away from baby's nose and mouth. Position the baby in the middle of the bed, between the adults, so that the baby can't roll out.

Toy safety. Only buy toys that are age appropriate. Virtually all new toys sold these days bear age labels, but you will need to be cautious about used toys purchased at yard sales. To be kept current on warnings about dangerous toys, subscribe to a parenting magazine, or read your daily newspaper with an eye out for stories about recalls of toys by the Consumer Product Safety Commission (CPSC). If you have access to the Internet on your computer, you can visit the CPSC's website at www.cpsc.gov and click on "recalls."

If you have a child who is under three and another who is three or over, make every effort to keep their toys separate. This is a very difficult task requiring constant watchfulness. Even a hyper-vigilant nanny may not be able to keep every single, tiny Lego piece out of a crawling baby's hands, and it only takes a split second for a toy to travel from hand to mouth. That's why it's essential for the nanny and parents alike to know the infant and child versions of the Heimlich maneuver.

Safety out of Doors

The number one rule in this area is that the nanny should not leave small children alone outside for any length of time. She must not

---

MY NANNY SAVED MY TODDLER FROM CHOKING ON A TOY

Ben, my younger son, used to love to play with this one toy truck that belonged to his older brother. It seemed to me rather sturdily built, and he had always played with it safely, so it hadn't occurred to us that he could pull the wheels off. One morning he was playing with the truck, putting his mouth around it as he often did, while I was getting ready to go off to work. My nanny, Carla, had just arrived. Somehow, when I wasn't looking, Ben had somehow managed to pull off both front wheels and the axle, and had got the whole assembly inside his mouth, with one wheel lodged partway down his throat. He wasn't breathing. Before I realized what was going on, my nanny was on top of him. She grabbed hold of one end of the wheel and axle that was sticking out of his mouth and with a single tug, got the other wheel to follow. After that I never let him play with his older brother's toys again. And I was more than grateful I had an observant nanny, too!

—Margaret from Washington, D.C.

run into the house "just for a minute" to answer the phone, but should instead let the answering machine pick up (or else take a portable phone outside with her). A fence around your yard should not induce a sense of complacency. Toddlers have been known to work their way under fences, as well as climb over—their need to explore is insatiable. Also, be aware that a child left in a yard alone is at risk for stranger abduction. Yes, such occurrences are rare, but they're not unheard of—and there's no reason at all for any child to be put at such risk.

In the garden. Instruct your nanny as to which, if any, plants in your garden pose a hazard to your child. Consult a gardening manual if need be. Make sure she can identify poison ivy, poison oak, and poison sumac and knows what to do in case of contact. For treatment of bee stings, it's a good idea to keep a first-aid kit within easy reach, because the faster the stinger can be extracted, the less severe the reaction will be. (Scraping with a plastic credit card may work, too.) She should know the signs of severe allergic reaction and know when to call 911.

Sandboxes. To prevent roaming cats from making a litter box in your backyard, keep your child's sandbox covered when not in use. If your child should play at a friends' house in a sandbox that's not kept covered, have the nanny wipe the child's hands afterward with an antiseptic wipe—especially if you are pregnant (or might become pregnant). Contact with contaminated sand can spread toxoplasmosis, a mild disease in itself, but one that can cause major birth defects if contracted in the second or third trimester of pregnancy.

On swingsets, slides, and other play structures. The most common danger is that a child will run too close in front of or behind other children who are swinging. This means that the nanny can't simply sit on a bench and watch while a small child plays; she should keep no more than a pace or two behind, close enough to swoop down and pull a child to safety, if need be. A good nanny will have a sense of whether a child is ready to handle a particular physical challenge. She will not assume, for example, that a two-year-old will be able to climb down from the monkey bars, just because he managed to get up there by himself. Safe parents and safe nannies reject the notion that letting a child fall and get hurt is the right way to teach her to know her own limits.

Pool safety. If you have a backyard pool, you should insist that your nanny be a strong swimmer. It would be wise for her to take and pass a water safety course, such as the American Red Cross lifeguard certification course. A swimming pool should always be kept inaccessible to small children, unless an adult is present. When the nanny takes your child to a community pool or neighbor's pool, *even if that pool is guarded*, the nanny must still assume primary responsibility for your child's safety. Even with children who can swim, the nanny must still be watchful, because it's always possible in a crowded pool for a child to get kicked in the head while swimming, become disoriented, and drown. With nonswimmers the rule should be that the child is only allowed in the water if the nanny (or some other responsible adult) gets in, too. Wading pools are no exception, as a child can drown in just two inches of water. Ring floats and waterwings may not be used as substitutes for an adult's supervision, since a child could slip out, or the device could puncture and deflate. When the nanny has to go to the bathroom, she must take the child with her, or else designate another adult to keep an eye on the child in her absence. This aspect of her performance is definitely something to spot check. Show up unexpectedly from work one summer day, and go directly to the pool when you know your nanny and child will be there. Observe silently for several minutes before you make your presence known. Let your nanny know right away if there is any improvement needed in her style of pool supervision.

Sun sense. During the spring and summer months, light-to-medium-complexioned children above the age of six months need sunscreen applied daily, and reapplied after swimming. The nanny should carry a bottle of long-lasting sunscreen with an SPF factor of 15 or more in her tote bag during all the high sunshine months of the year. Babies younger than six months should be kept covered by lightweight clothing and hats and kept in the shade as much as possible.

Driveway safety. Small children are more likely to be run over by a car backing out of their own driveway than they would almost anywhere else. Make sure your nanny understands that children are never allowed to play in the driveway, even when there is no car in sight. You never know when a car could pull in off the street, hunting for a place to make a quick turnaround. When loading several children in the car at once, always put the baby in first, keeping older ones by your side, until it is time to get them secured. Never permit children to wander behind a car with its engine on.

Street safety. When crossing the street, the nanny must be either holding the child's hand, carrying the child, or wheeling the child in a stroller. The nanny must strictly observe all the rules of pedestrian safety, crossing only at crosswalks, and never against the light, even if the street is deserted. It's important for her to set a good example, so that when the children are old enough to cross streets on their own, they'll have learned only good pedestrian habits.

Safety on the Go

Car safety. You checked into the nanny's safe driving record before hiring, but you still need to make sure she's familiar with your specific car(s), that she knows all the safety features, and uses them. Have her demonstrate for you the proper way to secure your child's safety seat, so that you're sure she's doing it right. Make it clear that she is never to start the car without checking to see that every seat belt is fastened. This rule is inviolable: It should be in force every time, on every trip, no matter how short. If asked to transport other children in your car, insist that there be a carseat or booster for every child small enough to need one. You do not want liability for an injury to an improperly secured child, even if the child's parent or nanny has given permission for the child to ride that way.

When the car is in motion, the nanny must never undo her own belt to retrieve a dropped pacifier or hand the baby a bottle. Anything that can't be done while belted requires pulling over and stopping.

In other vehicles. Safety is no less important in other vehicles than in your own car. If the nanny arranges for your child to be picked up for a play date in someone else's car, she should find out if the driver will provide your child with a carseat or booster seat; if not, the nanny must arrange to have the child's carseat or booster installed in the other car. The same goes for taxi rides, too. You may want to obtain a light, portable restraint, such as a seat-belt adjuster for children who weigh between forty and sixty pounds. Make sure children ride in the back seat only.

Emergency road procedures. You want your nanny to know what to do in case of an accident. She should know where the car's registration is kept, where to find insurance information, and how to get in touch with any emergency road service (such as AAA) that you are entitled to use. Carry in your trunk reflective triangles to signal that your vehicle is disabled. Your car should be equipped as well with a flashlight, a jack, and a lug wrench. Don't expect your nanny to be able to change a tire unassisted; those machine-fastened lug nuts may not come off under normal human power. If you live where it snows, carry some traction-adding substance such as sand or kitty litter, along with a snow shovel, an ice scraper, and a can of door lock de-icer. Make sure your nanny knows what all the dashboard dials and read-outs indicate, and that she keeps her eye on the gas gauge. You may want to give her a gasoline credit card so that she can fill up and charge gas to you when she needs to.

Bikes, trikes, ride-ons, skates, and sleds. It is up to the nanny to see to it every time a child gets on a bike that there is a helmet on that child's head. Tricycles and ride-on toys should be used only where safety can be assured, on quiet sidewalks, on playgrounds where permitted, and in other places where there is little or no likelihood of encountering cars. When in-line skates are used, more than a helmet is needed; the children should also wear knee pads, elbow pads, and gloves. Sledding accidents are an often overlooked but significant cause of emergency room admissions. Falling off a sled at high speed and hitting a tree can be every bit as deadly as skiing into one. (Recall the fate of Michael Kennedy and Sonny Bono as you instruct your nanny on this point.) Children must never be allowed to sled in wooded areas. Of course, there should be no sledding on or across streets.

Visits and outings. You've seen this scene before in the museum or at the shopping mall: There's a cute little toddler wandering around, seemingly on his own, until finally, you spot the adult, ambling along behind, entirely unconcerned. And you wonder, who are these irresponsible people, who let their kids roam around like so many stray cats? All too often, it's not a parent who's at fault, but a nanny. You want to know that your nanny will be different, that she will never allow your toddler to leave her line of sight. Ideally, she should walk hand in hand with the child, keeping a comfortable pace. She must never drag your child along by the elbow; neither should she let the child dawdle interminably. If the child for some reason balks at walking alongside her, then the nanny should be strong enough to pick the child up and carry him or her, if need be. Alternatively, she could bring along a stroller and insist the child stay in it.

On visits to friends' houses the nanny should not assume that any baby-proofing has been done but should keep a tight handle on the movements of your baby or toddler. Make sure your nanny asks your permission before she lets the nanny at the other house look after the children while she takes some time off. It's not unusual for nannies to make such arrangements with each other, and you may have no objection to the practice once you know the other nanny. You should make sure that the other set of parents are informed and are in agreement, too. Once such a practice is started, it can be of benefit to both families, as it increases the number of trusted caregivers you can call upon to fill in for you when faced with a childcare crisis.

NEVER FORGET THE NAME OF JAMES BULGAR

If anything could drive home the importance of keeping a small child within your sight while out in public, it is the story of two-year-old James Bulgar. He was walking with his mother at a shopping mall in England, when he momentarily slipped out of view. Within two minutes the toddler was spotted by two other boys, ages ten and eleven. The boys each grabbed hold of a hand and led him outside the shopping mall and then over to some train tracks, where they proceeded to beat him until he died.

Some Extra Safety Tips and Suggestions

Telephone Safety Tips

The following are some practices I highly recommend to increase your ability to contact your nanny in an emergency.

Cell phone. This is the number one safety extra I strongly recommend to nervous parents. With a little comparative shopping, you should be able to find a cell phone package that includes a small, foldable cellular phone, and a low monthly base rate with a reasonable charge per call. With a cell phone in her diaper bag, your nanny can call you wherever she happens to be, and more importantly, you can reach her when you need to. No more worrying about what might have happened when she and your child were expected back home at 6 P.M. and it's now close to 7. Cautions about not making calls or answering the phone while driving are in order. The nanny should always pull over first. If you are willing to spend a little extra on the model and the service, get a phone with a pager function, so that if she can't answer, you can leave your number and she can call you back when it's safe to do so. Cell phones offer other safety advantages: You have a way to get through even when your home phone is out of order, or the line to your street is down. And, if your car breaks down, the nanny can call for help.

To prevent having to pay for your nanny's personal use, you might stipulate that you will reimburse a set number of calls per month, and she is responsible for all others. Bills come with each call itemized, so that you can easily discriminate between work-related and non-work-related calls.

Telephone answering policy. Set and explain your policy on the first day of work regarding how and when your nanny should answer your phone. Make clear that looking after the children is always the number one priority. If she cannot safely get to the ringing telephone while she's busy with a child, she should let the answering machine pick up, and then play the message and return the call at her convenience.

One phone policy many parents adopt is to tell the nanny *never* to answer the phone during the workday. This, in my view, is a very unsafe approach. Parents argue that they do not want to make the nanny responsible for anything to do with the parents' private life or business dealings, and so do not want her to take messages for them. I say, if you can't trust your nanny to take a reliable phone message, how can you trust her with your child's care? The nanny should not be isolated and restricted from normal telephone usage. Quite the contrary, other nannies should be *encouraged* to call her during the workday and set up visits and play dates. In addition, the nanny should be expecting to get calls from you and your spouse on a regular basis, and consider it part of her job to converse with you when you call (unless, of course, she's in the middle of bathing a child or removing food from a hot burner at the moment the phone rings). Besides the initial check-up calls, parents will find they occasionally need to reach the nanny to reschedule a child's appointment or other activity, or that the school has called to ask that a sick child be picked up.

Tell the nanny that upon return home from an outing she should always play the answering machine messages as soon as she has a chance. For those intent on keeping a nanny from handling their business calls, the best solution is for you to install a separate business number, and instruct nanny not to answer that line.

Emergency numbers by *every* phone. Most parents keep a list of emergency numbers by one telephone—the one in the front hall, or the one in the kitchen. A safer policy is to copy the list of numbers and post it near every phone, or at a minimum, next to one phone on each level of the house. Numbers should be listed in order of use in time of emergency.

Your local emergency number should always come first (in most parts of the United States, it's 911), Second may be your pediatrician's office number (and off-hours number, if separate). I recommend listing the number of a poison control center third. When poisoning is suspected, a poison control center is the most reliable source of information and more knowledgeable than most pediatricians about the steps to be taken in response to the specific toxin that may have been ingested. To find out if your local area has a poison control center, check the front of your telephone directory. If none is listed, then use the twenty-four-hour number of the National Capital Poison Center, 202-623-3333, in Washington, D.C. Your emergency phone list may also include a number for a private ambulance service or volunteer rescue squad (particularly recommended for those who live in areas with substandard or slow-to-respond city or county emergency services). Next on the list are numbers to reach the parents during the day: main work numbers for each, followed by pager numbers and/or cell phone numbers. You should also provide numbers of nearby neighbors, especially any that you know are usually home during the workday. Other frequently used numbers you might want to list are: child's school, teacher's home number, grandparents' houses, houses of friends frequently visited.

Very Important: Your phone list should always include your street address, plus simple directions to get there from the nearest major street. I once attended a safety lecture by the head of a local emergency response team. The lecturer said that sitters and nannies who call for an ambulance frequently are unable to say exactly where they are calling from. Not every emergency response system includes a computerized telephone locator program. To save precious time when every second counts, make sure the caller does not have to stop to look up any information when speaking to the emergency dispatcher.

Memorize important numbers. The emergency phone list is mainly intended to be of use when you have left your children with an occasional sitter for the evening. Your regular nanny should not have to look up important numbers during an emergency. The first day she starts to work, she should be given a list of numbers to memorize. By the end of the first week you should be confident that she knows by heart your work number, your spouse's work number, and the pager and/or cell phone numbers for each of you. Be sure if a number is changed that she is kept current and is reminded to memorize the new number promptly.

TIP: MAKE AN EMERGENCY WALLET CARD

After you have compiled your list of emergency numbers, type it up on a computer using a very small point size (8 or 9 point, for most type styles). If you have room, add other emergency information, such as health insurance policy number, and any medical conditions you would like an emergency-room physician to know about. Print out the list onto a piece of paper, and then cover it with a credit card. Trace around the edges, and then take a scissors and cut out the card-sized list. Go to a drugstore or an art supply store to buy laminating plastic. Cover the front and back of the card, and then trim the plastic to just beyond the edges of the card. You now have a durable, wallet-sized emergency card for your nanny to keep with her at all times. I made one for the nanny to keep in the diaper bag, plus one for my wife, and one for myself.

—Bill from Washington, D.C.

Miscellaneous Medical and Safety Tips

Keep first-aid kits in the kitchen, car, diaper bag, and backpack. Your nanny's excellent training in first aid is useless if she doesn't have ready access to supplies. Every house needs a well-stocked first-aid kit that organizes all the essential supplies in one place. Do not store the kit in any room with high humidity (such as a bathroom). Because the kitchen is one of the most common places for accidents to occur, a good choice would be in a safety-latched kitchen cabinet. For a comprehensive list of what should go in your first-aid kit, buy a good, clear, easy-to-check home medical reference book. (The American Pediatric Association puts out an excellent, comprehensive guide.) Smaller, lighter kits can be assembled and kept in the trunk of your car(s) or underneath the seat(s); be sure to include one in your diaper bag, totebag, or backpack to have on hand at any outing.

Children with special medical needs. Special precautions should be taken for children with a potentially life-threatening medical condition.

EMERGENCY INFORMATION

Ambulance	911
Bethesda Vol. Rescue Squad	301-652-1000
Kids' doctor	301-555-3456
Dentist	301-555-9999
Bill's office	202-555-6789
Peggy's office	202-555-9876
Cell phone	202-555-4321
Peggy's cell phone	202-555-5656

Health Insurance #000-11-2222 group#1234

Sarah has allergy to bee stings
Richard is allergic to penicillin

If a child has an allergy that is known to cause anaphylactic shock (breathing difficulties due to swelling of the windpipe), the nanny should have ready access to an EpiPen, Jr., a measured dose of injectible epinephrine. Ask your child's allergist or pediatrician to write you a prescription for a minimum of three such devices: one to be kept at home, one to be kept in the nanny's totebag for outings, and one to be kept at the child's school. Children with asthma should also be supplied with an inhaler to have easily accessible at all times in case of an asthma attack. Parents of children with diabetes, epilepsy, or any other medical condition requiring regular medication should make sure that the nanny knows how and when to administer the dosage of the specific medication the child requires. A nanny who takes care of a child with a serious medical condition should receive special training to be able to recognize and respond to the specific type or types of emergency that child may experience.

In case the nanny has a medical emergency. Suppose the nanny should slip and fall and become unconscious. A child as young as two can be taught to call for help. The fastest, easiest way to teach the child to call for help is to instruct him or her to pick up the telephone and dial 0. The child can just say, "Help!" or can try to explain what has happened to the nanny. Operators are trained to contact 911 or your local emergency service when a child is on the line under such circumstances. Dialing a single digit, 0, is much easier for a child to remember and perform correctly than remembering three separate digits, 9-1-1, and accurately hitting the numbers. If you have a telephone with speed-dial buttons, you might label them in a way your small child can understand. One button might be a speed-dial connection to Mom's office, with a small photo of Mom taped beside it; another button might have Dad's picture, and perhaps one with a red cross on it to symbolize an ambulance. Other buttons may be programmed to call someone on whom you know you can count for emergency assistance, such as a neighbor or a relative.

Answering the door. There is no good reason for your nanny ever to open the door of your home to a stranger. Unknown persons could just be selling door to door, or passing out religious literature, or raising money for a good cause . . . or they could be burglars looking to overpower a woman who is alone in a house with children . . . or worse. It should not be up to your nanny to judge the character of the person who rings your doorbell, whether in darkness or in the light of day. The rule should be inflexible: "Do not open the door of this house to any person unknown to you." You should, of course, introduce her to your neighbors and your close friends. However, if someone comes to the door claiming to be a friend of yours, or perhaps the parent of a friend of your child, no matter how innocent they may look through the peephole or through the window, your nanny should remain on her own side of the locked door. She may want to use the following line: "I'm sorry, but this house has a strictly enforced policy of not opening the door to people unless we're expecting them." She may add, "You can leave a note at the door, or if you prefer, you can call Sally's mom or dad at work and let them set up a visit on another day."

Persons claiming to need help in an emergency should be told by the nanny (through the locked door) that she will make a telephone call on their behalf to summon assistance. She can then call the police, fire department, or ambulance, as needed—but she should not agree to make any additional calls, until the authorities arrive.

Because it's usually awkward to conduct a conversation through a locked door, homeowners who are concerned about security may want to have a doorbell intercom, or perhaps even a front-door videotaping system installed. You can spend as much as several thousand dollars for a state-of-the-art system or as little as about $40 for a pair of wired, station-to-station intercoms that you can find in any home electronics store.

Alarm system. If you do not have a home security system already, consider having one installed. A well-designed system will do more than help guard your property against burglars, but may also include the following features:

- a panic alarm to summon help immediately, when there is no time to talk
- a hostage code, so that you can silently let the alarm company know that you are face to face with an intruder
- a smoke alarm that automatically alerts the alarm system's monitoring center, which will in turn inform your local fire department of the exact location of the fire in your house

Fire safety. Every house should have at least one smoke detector on every level. The nanny should know how to recognize the "low-battery" warning beeps, and be shown how to change the batteries. Every family should have a fire escape plan, including how to escape from upper levels when stairs or doors become blocked. A foldable chain fire escape ladder that can be kept stored in an upper floor closet is a worthwhile purchase (see the Resource Guide in the back of this book for toll-free numbers of catalogs that carry this product). Make the point as you go over fire safety procedures that you do not want your nanny to do anything other than get the children out safely. She isn't responsible for pets or valuables, nor should she permit the children to gather up any toys or favorite blankets. Children, as soon as they are old enough to understand, should begin learning fire-safe procedures themselves. They should be taught never to hide during a fire, but to do exactly what the adult in charge tells them to do. If a child sees smoke, the child should alert an adult. Do *not* train your small child to stop to call 911—the child's only concern should be to get out of the house. If there is too much smoke to see the way out, the children should crawl along floor, feeling their way toward the nearest exit.

Other safety features. Safety-conscious parents might also consider the following devices:

Carbon monoxide detector: Like a smoke detector, this simple early detection device sounds an alarm when toxic levels of carbon monoxide build up. Carbon monoxide is a colorless, odorless gas that can build up because of a malfunctioning or improperly vented furnace, space heater, gas fireplace, wood stove, or other combustion-producing appliance.

Automatic sprinkler system: Many newer homes have this life-saving feature. If a fire starts, ceiling sprinklers automatically turn on and spray water, putting out the fire before it can spread. If you'll be doing extensive remodeling or putting on an addition, investigate the possibility of "retro-fitting" to install ceiling sprinklers at the same time the other construction work is done. Be sure to discuss your plan with your home insurance company, because most policies offer a significant discount in premiums for homes with this feature.

Flood detector: This device emits a warning sound if the basement becomes flooded due to a pipe break, storm, washing machine overflow, or other cause of excess water. Your home security system may offer the device as an add-on to the rest of the system, in which case the central monitoring service will send for help if the alarm should be triggered when no one is at home. You may also purchase the device through a home safety catalog (see the Resource Guide at the back of this book for catalog titles and toll-free numbers) or at certain hardware stores. The device may also be called a "water monitor" or a "water bug."

Your nanny should become familiar with each type of safety monitor in your house, be able to identify any sort of warning noise she hears, and know how you want her to respond in each situation.

Correcting Safety Mistakes

Let's say you've just found out the nanny has been letting your baby ride on her lap in a taxi, even though you thought you had made clear that your child has to be in her carseat any time she's in a moving vehicle. You are not about to fire the nanny over the incident, because on the whole you've been pleased with her care of your child—but on the other hand, you want to be sure she understands she has made a serious mistake. More importantly, you want to be certain that she will

---

**SAFETY FACTOID: CARBON MONOXIDE IS A
SILENT KILLER**

Carbon monoxide buildup in a guest cottage where tennis star
Vitas Gerulaitas was staying killed him in his sleep. A $30 carbon
monoxide detector could have saved his life.

---

follow your instructions explicitly on this point in the future. You don't
want her to think that she can continue to do without a carseat, as
long as you don't find out. How should you get the point across?

You could, of course, threaten to fire her for one more such safety
violation, and she might well comply with your order out of fear for
her job—but she still won't believe in her heart that your safety instructions make sense. For you to have full confidence that she will do things
the safe way every time (and not just when there's a chance you could
catch her), you want her to see the necessity of the rule herself. The
way to persuade her is to empathize with her view of the situation,
but then let her hear a true story that makes clear what the real-life
consequences have been for others who have done things her way.
Adopt a self-deprecating tone as you tell her the story, so that she can
see you're not perfect either—just trying to do the best you can for
your baby. Never lecture or scold.

Your story might go something like this [the story is based upon
an actual incident that occurred in Florida in the 1980s]:

> You know, I used to think it was okay for a baby to ride on a
> lap for a short distance myself. Then, a few years ago, I heard
> a story on the news that made me rethink the idea. The story
> was about a family with a baby about the same age as Allie.
> The baby had been sick, and the dad was driving him to the
> corner drugstore to pick up his prescription. Because he had
> been so fussy that day, he didn't want to go in his carseat, so
> the mom thought it would be okay, just that one time, and

just for a few blocks, to hold him on her lap, under her own seatbelt. Well, the dad was making a left turn on the arrow, when another car ran the light at high speed and hit them on the passenger side. The adults survived the crash, but the mother's seatbelt didn't hold the baby, who went flying through the windshield and was killed. On top of this tragedy of losing their son, both parents were charged with criminal negligence for failure to have their child in a carseat.

If, after listening to your story, the nanny still seems defensive or if she disputes the meaning of the example you have chosen, then you are on notice that she does not assign safety the same priority as you, and you should be concerned. You might need to start doing some spot-checks to be sure your instructions are being carried out.

CHAPTER EIGHT

PROBLEM SOLVING

Time out of Mind

Dear Nanny Advisor:

Dolly is in many ways a wonderful nanny, but she's always running late. She arrives somewhere between five to forty-five minutes after her start time in the morning, and in the afternoon, more than a few times she has shown up so late at my daughter's school that the principal has had to call me. We've reminded her and lectured her, but we're at wit's end. Should we let her go? Our children love her.

> Signed,
> Father Time

Dear Daddy-T:

Here's my solution: Set her official start-time a half hour earlier in the morning than you really need her. Tolerate lateness of up to twenty minutes past her new official start time, but if she's consistently a half hour late or more (and it happens more than once a week), then it's clear she's not even making an effort, and you probably will have to get rid of her.

The school pick-up problem is a trickier thing to deal with. You might try buying her a digital watch with several different alarms you can set. Have the first reminder alarm go off well in advance of the time she needs to get ready to leave for school. Set a follow-up alarm to go off about ten minutes later. Then have a final warning beep to let her know that she's got to be on her way. Ask a teacher, another nanny, or a parent to keep on eye on things and let you know if the late pick-up problem is still going on. If the answer is yes, you will have to decide whether to fire her, or you'll need to find some way to relieve her of this one responsibility that she seems unable to meet. Is there a school bus your child can take? Is there another parent who would, perhaps for reasonable recompense, be willing to bring your daughter home each day? You could also look for a bonded and insured child-taxi service to do the job. (Most large metropolitan areas have them—check your telephone directory.)

The Case of the Disappearing References

Dear Nanny Advisor:

I'm thinking of making a job offer to a nanny, Lisa, who seems very caring and responsible. The trouble is, she has no references that I can trust. Her previous employer's company went belly-up, and the family fled the area, leaving no forwarding address—though a horde of creditors apparently are trying to track them down. I know this is true because there was a write-up about it in the newspaper. Before that, Lisa worked for a woman whose notions of good childcare are totally different from my own. She had Lisa working horribly long days, from 7:30 A.M. to 8:45 P.M., and she screamed at Lisa when the children's toys were ever left out in their rooms. She wanted Lisa to spank the children over trivial mistakes. So Lisa finally quit in disgust. Even if this employer would give Lisa a decent reference, I'm not sure I would give much weight to her opinion. Lisa is twenty-one, and her only other full-time jobs have been as a waitress and as a summer camp counselor. How should I proceed?

> Signed
> Past Imperfect

Dear P.I.:

Definitely try to track down someone in charge of the sum-mer camp where Lisa worked. That reference should be able to give you an idea of how patient and careful Lisa was with the children, whether she ever lost her temper, whether she took direction well, and other information you need. Also, has Lisa been doing any evening or weekend babysitting over the past few years? If she's sat for the same family at least three times, ask her to give you that family's number as a reference. Two or three such references should be able to fill in the picture pretty well. If she can't provide even these kinds of short-term references, I'd be concerned. Perhaps she lacks the experience you need in a nanny. In addition to seeking out more references, I would certainly schedule a couple of prac-tice-sits—hiring Lisa to watch your children for an evening or on a Saturday afternoon, while you stay in the house. If you're satisfied with what you see, then go ahead and make her an offer. Nothing is as convincing as the evidence of your own eyes and ears, in any case.

A Job Up in Smoke?

Dear Nanny Advisor:

When I interviewed Renate, I knew that, like a lot of Euro-pean girls, she was a smoker, but she promised me she would quit before she started work. While I've never seen evidence of cigarettes in the house, my husband happened to catch a glimpse of her after work one evening, sitting with some friends in an outdoor café—and Renate, like all the rest of them, was smoking. I asked her directly if she had started smoking again, and she told me she had only meant to say that she would not smoke while around the kids. Should I accept that answer, or should I insist that she give up cigarettes completely?

Signed,

Hazy about the Future

Dear Haze:

To decide that question you may want to consider the following factors:

Is she a live-in? I would not allow someone to reside in my house who was, inside my house or out, a smoker. I would always be worried that she might leave a pack of matches where my child could get hold of them, or sneak a cigarette in bed one night and fall asleep with the embers still burning.

Are you providing her with health insurance? In that case, she must have checked off nonsmoker on the application form. If she has filled out the form untruthfully, she has put you at financial risk, and you will need to take steps to correct the situation.

Is your child old enough to know what smoking is and to look to the nanny as a role model? With any child over the age of three who is likely to encounter the nanny in her free time, you don't want to have to explain why the nanny is seen doing something your child should be taught to regard as both dangerous and dumb.

However, if the nanny lives out, is not covered by a health insurance policy that you pay for, and your child is too young for the role model question to come up, then I would say (assuming, of course, that she has in other regards been a good nanny) don't get all fired up about this issue. Just make it absolutely clear that smoking around your children is forbidden at all times.

Olfactory Blues

Dear Nanny Advisor:

I like my new nanny's personality, I like her energy and hardworking attitude. There's only one thing I've found about her that I don't really like: her smell. I don't know if her B.O. comes from not bathing enough, or maybe she needs a stronger deodorant, but we've all noticed it . . . even my five-year-old son! Should I anonymously mail her a bottle of a good, strong roll-on? Or tell her flat out that she has a problem?

> Signed,
> Miss Rose

Dear Rosie:

Your first suggestion is too subtle. Someone else in her family may take the hint meant for her (and maybe they need it, too). Your second course of action is too blunt, and she might become so embarrassed that she'll quit. This situation calls for the right euphemisms, plus a little polite fictionalizing to avoid giving offense. What you need to do is put the blame on yourself. Tell her the problem is with you, that you've got this condition of hypersensitivity, which makes you react with a rash or a runny nose to people who use certain personal care products. So it's very important to you to be sure that she showers every morning with a particular brand of soap that you find nonreactive. (Hand her any brand of soap you like, so long as it's labeled "hypoallergenic".) Tell her she must also be sure to use a particular brand of deodorant in the morning, as well. (Hand her a strong brand, and don't worry about what it says on the label.) If the problem persists, repeat your explanation of your extreme sensitivity, and emphasize how important it is for her to do what she can to help you cope with your problem. If after the second talk on the subject, things haven't improved, then it seems clear that she's not going to make an effort on your behalf—so the next call is up to you. If you really can't stand it . . . you know what you have to do.

Boyfriend Trouble

Dear Nanny Advisor:

Stella has been a fine nanny, but she lacks good taste in men. Her latest boyfriend is a horror. He's unemployed, unshaven, uses bad language, and we're pretty sure he runs around on her. As a consequence, she's often moody and mopey. Our hope is she'll break up with him, once and for all. She seems to realize he's no good, but just can't seem to work up the courage to tell him off. Sometimes I get the feeling she's waiting for us to give her the incentive she needs. I'd love to do just that, but my husband says "back off." Who's right?

> Signed,
> Ann Landers Wannabe

Dear Wannabe:

Your husband is right. Telling the nanny to make her boy-friend take a hike runs a high risk of having her decide to try out the opposite course of action, just to assert her independence. If she's looking for a shoulder to cry on, provide it—but be a girlfriend, not a mom. Talk about your own experiences, if you like, but don't force any conclusions on her, and definitely don't order her around! When she feels supported and loved and is shown that you trust her good sense, she will feel better equipped to demand such treatment from others—including this bum. With some patience and forbearance on your part, this guy should not be around too much longer.

Boyfriend Trouble II

Dear Nanny Advisor:

Okay, I ignored your advice. I told Stella in no uncertain terms to dump the creep . . . and she did (and she didn't seem to resent me for saying so). So that problem is solved—but now I have a more difficult problem. The creep won't give up. He's been calling her ten to twenty times a day. When my husband told him to stop calling, the creep threatened to come over and do something to him. He's cursed at me so often, I'm terrified to answer the phone. I'm afraid for my children, if he should show up one day and become violent. What should I do now?

Signed,
Scared (former Wannabe)

Dear Scared:

Now Stella's problem really *is* your problem, and your children's problem, too. The time has come to put their safety first. Stella needs to consider her own safety, as well, which is far more important than her job security. The guy sounds obsessed, and there is every indication that he could be turning into a stalker. Don't wait for that to happen, or look to anti-stalking laws to help. (Real fanatics just ignore those re-

straining orders from the court.) Do everything you can to see
to it that Stella gets a new job as soon as possible, and for
everyone's sake, as far away as possible. Of course, keep her
new whereabouts a secret. Report the harassing calls to the
telephone company and the police, and follow the advice you
receive about monitoring the calls or changing your number.
Take the threat very seriously. There have actually been a few
cases of murder committed by an enraged ex-boyfriend at the
home where the ex-girl friend worked as a nanny.

The Nanny Who Came "Out"

Dear Nanny Advisor:

My husband and I are religious and quite traditional in our
views of family life. The nanny we hired—I'll call her "Ellen"—
seemed, at the time, to share our values and outlook. Now,
three years later, she has come to us saying she has finally discovered her "true self." She says she is a lesbian. We are not
at all comfortable with this revelation. She lives out, so we
never had any way of knowing what she did in her private
life . . . and we wish we still didn't know. Our daughters are
two and six, and they love her very much. What's your reading
of this situation?

Signed,
No Sitcom

Dear No Sit:

My reading is that your nanny would have been better off
not trying to involve you in such a private matter. Since her
sexual orientation has absolutely no bearing on the way she
does her job, and she is aware of your discomfort over the issue,
she should have known better than to burden you with her
confidence. But now that the news is "out," don't compound
her mistake by dwelling on it. Treat the matter as you say you
wish it had remained: private, and entirely her own business.
If she brings the subject up again, tell her that you believe her

personal life is an inappropriate subject for her to bring up at work. Put an air of finality in your voice as you say this. (By the way, I sense, from your mention of your children's age and gender, some possible concern for their safety with a lesbian for a sitter. If she has never given you reason to worry about her conduct toward them before, there's no cause for worry now.)

Breakable Objects

Dear Nanny Advisor:

Adjoining the master bedroom in our house is a little study that contains an antique desk, and above it, some glass shelves holding a few fragile, and quite expensive objects. On her very first day of work we instructed our nanny that this room is strictly off limits to the children. One day last week I came home to find a small ceramic elephant shattered in a hundred pieces on the floor. It was a wedding present from my great-uncle who has since passed away; he had brought it back from Cambodia over forty years ago, and so it held great sentimental value to me, as well as monetary value. The only ones home all day were the nanny and my three-year-old twin boys. I asked the nanny how the accident had occurred, and she professed surprise to hear that anything was broken. Neither she nor the boys had been in the room all day—so she told me. There was no wiggle-room in her denial, and yet no other way that I can figure out how anything could have been broken. (We have no pets, and there's been no seismic activity that could have caused anything to shake off the shelves.)

I am very disturbed by this incident. In truth, although I was angry over the breakage at the time, I'm sure I would have forgiven her if she'd just explained how it had happened. Now I'm all confused, and not sure I can trust her. Please advise.

Signed,
Shattered

Dear Shattered:

You've got to shift your focus from the small pieces to the big picture. Stand back from the incident and let a bit of time pass by, to allow you to collect your thoughts. Now consider the overall situation. Ask yourself: Is your distrust of her limited to this one thing, or is it a general loss of faith in her character? Do you think she's no longer a safe and loving caretaker for your sons? If so, listen to your gut, and let her go (because you'll never feel really comfortable working with her again). Now, if you're just not able to fully trust her account of this one incident—but you believe she would never lie to you about anything concerning your children's health or safety, then I don't recommend such a drastic response. I would sit down with her and say something along these lines:

"I know you say you weren't aware that the elephant had broken. I'm not questioning your word, but I need to let you know that it disturbs me that something could have come crashing down in the house while you were here, and you didn't at least hear it. Fortunately, though, it's just a thing, not a person, so it's not that important, when you think about it. What *does* matter to me is to know that I can count on you to come to me, openly, without hesitation, and tell me what's happening at home, whether good or bad. I think I'm a pretty understanding person and can deal with the fact that accidents can happen." [Pause to allow her to add any new information on how the breakage could have occurred, if she is so inclined. If she says nothing, go on:] "Well, anyway, I don't want to let this one thing create any sort of problem between us, so let that be the last we'll talk about it."

It won't, of course, be the last time you'll *think* about it. It may take some time for her to work her way back up to the level of confidence you had in her before the breakage occurred. And I would definitely buy a lock for that study door.

And Baby Makes Four

Dear Nanny Advisor:

My nanny is pregnant. She and her husband hadn't been planning to have a baby quite so soon (they've been married for less than a year) but she's still quite happy about it, and my children are excited about it, too. I'm afraid I'm the only one who's less than thrilled. She says she'd like to take off for just a week or two after the delivery, and then bring her baby to work with her, but I'm not sure I like that idea. A newborn requires such a high level of attention, it seems to me that my own children will end up getting far less of her time than they need (and far less than I'm paying for). Also, I think once she actually has the baby, she'll realize she wants to spend more time at home with the baby, and will delay coming back to work. I will end up scrambling to find fill-ins for an unknown number of weeks. My husband, meanwhile, tells me I'm a worry-wart, and reminds me that she's always been good on her word. I say he's a man, and he's never given birth. What do you say?

Signed
ZPG

Dear Gee:

I'm with you. You didn't take her on with a shared-nanny plan in mind. If that's not what you want for your children, then don't be boxed into it. Be frank with her. You're not a large corporation and so you can't be held to standards set for rich companies when it comes to giving extended family leave. Do your best to work out a compromise that allows her reasonable time off, but if she chooses to come back to work, she's got to arrange childcare for her baby—just as you do.

Feeding Frenzy

Dear Nanny Advisor:

I'm breastfeeding my baby, and I want her to have only my breastmilk in bottles, and nothing else when I'm away at work. I spend much of my free time pumping, so that I always have a good supply in the freezer for my nanny to thaw, bottle, and feed to my daughter when she's hungry. At first I thought my nanny was supportive of my feeding program, but lately she's been pressuring me to let her supplement with formula. She told me that my baby was fussy a lot after a bottle, and she thought that meant the baby was still hungry. I held firm, and after a while she stopped bringing the matter up. I thought that meant the end of the issue, but then one day after the nanny had gone home, I was cleaning up after supper when I noticed an empty single-serve can of ready-to-eat formula in the trash. I asked my nanny about it, and she admitted, yes, she'd been feeding my baby formula, at her own expense, for weeks. I'm furious, and I really want to fire her, but my husband says she was only acting in what she believed to be the baby's best interest. He points out that the baby really is a whole lot less fussy since she's been getting the supplements. He even got the pediatrician to talk to me, to tell me that supplementing was indicated, since the baby is older now and needs more bottles than I was able to provide. Even so, I'm still upset. Do you think I'm blowing this out of proportion?

Signed,
Double-D

Dear DeeDee:

No, you're not. The real issue here is not breastmilk versus formula, but trust versus deception. You set down certain feeding instructions, which you trusted the nanny to carry out. She failed to do that, and then she lied, at least by omission, by leading you to believe that the matter had been resolved to your satisfaction. This is not a problem to be treated lightly. A

responsible nanny might still have her own opinion about feeding, but she would do her best to impress you with her daily
observations about the baby's feeding pattern and then she
would discuss with you any change she believed was in order.
She would never resort to taking action behind your back.
Think of the implications of her actions for the future: Suppose
one week your child is supposed to be given medication according to a certain schedule. How can you be sure that your
nanny will follow the doctor's instructions, and then report to
you accurately about what she did? See if you can get your
husband to focus on that issue, and quit arguing over the contents of the bottle.

Give Me That Old-time Religion

Dear Nanny Advisor:

Our nanny, Marianne, is a member of a fundamentalist
Christian church, and we are not Christian. She has never
done anything like take our children to church behind our
backs, or try to inculcate them in her faith; the problem is
more subtle than that. She lives in, and for the past five years
she has been extremely close to our daughter, Susan, who is
now eight. (Our other child, a son, is just one.) Susan is becoming more and more curious about Marianne's religious practices, and we fear, is attracted to the idea of converting. We've
never tried to discourage Marianne from answering questions
about her religion before, or objected to all the religious jewelry
she wears around her neck during the workday. We never
minded before that she kept a Christmas tree and a nativity
scene in her room from mid-October to the end of January, or
that she enlisted Susan's help in decorating the tree and setting
up the creche. But now that Susan has expressed an interest
in changing to Marianne's faith, we're wondering if we should
have applied the brakes a little sooner. We're really not sure
what to do right now. Would we be within our rights to tell
Marianne to refer all religious inquiries back to us? (Please
don't suggest we sign Susan up for instruction in our own faith.

My husband and I are not members of any organized religious institution, and have no interest in joining.)
Signed
Agnostic

Dear Aggie:

Your daughter's desire to imitate the practices of the person she loves and admires is a perfectly normal and even a touching sign of love. Since Marianne is not doing anything to impose her own beliefs on your child, I wouldn't put the onus on her to stifle her normal religious expression (especially when it comes to personal adornment or the decoration of her own room). You say you have enjoyed a long and stable relationship with her; in that case, show some trust in her judgment and allow her to answer your daughter's questions about her faith in the way she thinks best. At the same time, you, as a parent, have an even longer history of mutual love and respect with your daughter. She needs to know what you think and why. Spend as much time with her as you need to while you explain to her why you see things in a different light. Be careful not to belittle Marianne's beliefs or set yourself up in competition with her faith for your daughter's loyalty. Reassure her that she will be allowed, within certain reasonable limits, to satisfy her curiosity and try out various practices—but you will probably want to draw the line at conversion. Given a little leeway and time, your daughter will, in all likelihood, complete her experimentation with Marianne's religion, and after that phase is done, will return to your own way of looking at religion . . . and you won't be out a good nanny in the process.

Screaming Fits

Dear Nanny Advisor:

My nine-month-old girl Janna doesn't do well with new people or situations. She has horrible screaming bouts every morning as I prepare to leave for work, and she covers her face and cries as soon as the nanny appears. It's been more than a week, and she shows no signs of getting over her separation anxiety and adjusting to her new routine. I've been a stay-at-home mom till now, but I had been looking forward to getting back to work. I had not been prepared for the strength of her reaction. What's worse, I'm not entirely sure if Janna is really any better during the day. The nanny assures me that she settles down after the first ten or fifteen minutes, and then she's fine until I come home. I have performed a few spot-checks, and Janna does seem to be okay, but then the instant she sees me, she clings to me, and starts crying and wailing all over again. I have no way of telling whether she's crying because she really dislikes the nanny, or is still reacting to the fact that I'm not at home with her anymore. Also, whenever I've come home for a spot-check, it's been practically impossible for me to leave Janna for the second time to return to work. So there I am, stuck at home for the rest of the day, and having to pay for a nanny, too! I'm wondering if all this agony is worth it. Should I be handling things differently? And what about the nanny's role?

> Signed,
> Guilt-Ridden Rita

Dear GRR:

Nine months *is* a difficult age. Your baby is old enough to be aware that you are a separate individual, old enough to recognize that the pattern of her life has changed, old enough to experience the fear that you may not return—but still too young to understand your reassurances, and too young to communicate her fear by any other means except screaming. In all likelihood, her reaction to the nanny's arrival has nothing to do with that particular nanny's behavior and everything to do with your child's age, personality, and habits. Still, you need more than a sense of "in all likelihood" to have peace of mind. Since your own spot-checks simply get the separation anxiety started up again, you need to employ a substitute whose judgment you trust. Do you have a close friend or relative who could stop by your house a few times during the initial period and report to you accurately on how your baby and the nanny seem to be getting on?

You can also get something of a sense of how things are going yourself, through frequent telephone calls at varying times of the day. Unless you hear your baby crying or wailing in the background each time you call, you should relax and reassure yourself that the baby really does settle down after a while. One week is not a long time for a baby to balk at a new arrangement. If the screaming at the changeover continues un-abated for another two or three weeks, then it's time to start experimenting with ways to make the transition less traumatic for her. You might try establishing a more gradual good-bye ritual in the mornings, or perhaps go for the opposite approach, and use a shorter, more abrupt one. You might want to con-sider a morning leave-taking ritual that bypasses you alto-gether: That is, have your spouse handle the transition from parental care to nanny-care, while you slip out of the house unnoticed. Tailor your actions to what you know about your own child; be creative; be watchful for signs of progress; but most of all, be patient. One day you *will* get to the point where transition becomes an accepted part of her daily routine. Of course, when that happens, she will probably have fallen in love with the nanny, and then you will one day undoubtedly experience the problem discussed below.

Too Much Loyalty

Dear Nanny Advisor:

Our children, two and five, have had the same nanny, Ruth, since they were born. Now she tells us she'll be leaving us to go back to Jamaica for good. She has helped us find a replace-ment, who seems every bit as good, but the problem is that the children just can't seem to accept the idea. When we had the new nanny over to do a practice baby-sitting session, both chil-dren cried and asked why they had to have anyone other than Ruth. Our two-year-old boy shouted rude things at the new nanny and hid, and had to be dragged out from under the bed. Our five-year-old girl says bluntly, "It's no use trying to make me like her. I'll never like anyone but Ruth." I'm beginning to think this is true. What do you think?

Signed,

Benedict Arnold

Dear Benny:

I've got a few ideas for you to try. Bribery, for example. It's crude, it's not to be defended in philosophical terms—but it usually works. Have the new nanny arrive one morning bearing some wonderful presents you know your kids really will love. Before you let them unwrap anything, however, make sure they understand that the gifts are from the new nanny, and that she picked them out because she wanted to see the children smile when she came. You may need to repeat the bribery a few more times before your kids start to loosen up.

Another approach is for you to stop playing the bad guy and let Ruth assume her fair share of the burden. Have her give them a talking-to—gently but firmly. She should tell them that the new nanny is a friend of hers, and that it hurts her feelings (Ruth's, that is) when she hears that they've been rude to her friend. She should make clear to the children that she is going to leave, whether they accept the fact or not, but it would make her very sad to leave things on such an unhappy note. She will feel much better if she can leave, knowing that everyone is getting along. Your children may more easily accept the reality of the situation coming from Ruth than from you.

One thing you definitely want to do is to reassure them that by loving the new nanny they do not take anything away from Ruth. Reassure them frequently that Ruth will still love them as much, even though she's far away. Talk to them about how they will be able to keep in touch with her through telephone calls and letters. Make sure you follow through, by keeping up the contact that you have promised.

Let the new nanny work her own magic, as well. Encourage her to come up with some fun activities for the kids to do. If

she's a good nanny, she will have some creative ideas. She'll
also be patient and gentle while waiting for your children to
adjust . . . which they will, in time. I say this from experience,
having put my own children through some extremely difficult
nanny changes, and having seen them survive (even though
there were a few tearful days when I wasn't quite sure they
would).

Not the Best of Friends

Dear Nanny Advisor:

We have no complaint about how our nanny looks after the
children. She is perfectly good at caring for them and playing
with them, and they love her. Our only complaint is that *we*
don't particularly like her. She's a sweet and inoffensive person,
but we just don't enjoy her company. She lives in, and she
seems to have no social life with friends her own age, so she's
always around. Any suggestions?

Signed,

Distant

Dear Diss:

Is there any possibility that she could live out? That way you
would not have to concern yourself so much with the quality
of her social life. If that's not a possibility, then just do what
you can to encourage her to get out more. Tell her that you
want to see her have some fun, exercise her independence, and
go out and enjoy herself. It may help for you to consider *why*
you don't enjoy her company. Maybe it's because she's intimidated by you, and she feels she has nothing to talk about with
you. In that case it might be worthwhile for you to help her to
pursue her education, take some college-level courses, to
broaden her horizons. Taking an interest in her as a person
will be good for both sides.

Another, different approach to the problem is not to get to
know her better, but to establish sharper boundaries between

you, so that your relationship with her is mainly that of an employer, not as housemates. See if you can bring about a more apartmentlike separation between your part of the house and hers. Does she have her own cooking facilities? If not, you might want to add some appliances that would give her the ability to handle her own food preparation, so that you won't always be dining together. Make sure she has her own entertainment, including CD player, TV, and VCR. Make sure she knows she's allowed to have guests over. You might even offer to supply a babysitter some night, and go out, vacating the house so that she can give a dinner party. Anything you can do to help her develop her own social life will be a plus. Once she realizes that there's more she can do with herself than hang around the house with her employers, she'll be happier, too. And when your nanny is happy, everybody benefits.

CONCLUSION

To sum up, I have compiled a list of the most important rules and safety precautions for nanny hiring found within this book. I call these "The Ten Commandments of the Safe Nanny Search." Follow these faithfully, and you may be able to find a nanny who is a true angel from heaven.

The Ten Commandments of the Safe Nanny Search

I. Take your time. A safe nanny is never found in haste.

II. Always have a back-up childcare plan. You don't want to have to accept someone just because you've got nothing else you can do with your kids. They deserve better than the nanny of last resort.

III. Make your job package as good as you can, to attract the highest quality of candidate available.

IV. Prescreen rigorously by phone. Don't waste precious time interviewing someone who can't communicate effectively over the phone or who doesn't meet your advertised requirements.

V. Interview extensively. Forty-five minutes covering all aspects of the job is the minimum recommended time. That doesn't include the house tour and the meeting with your children.

VI. Listen to your gut. If there's something that just doesn't feel right to you about a nanny, don't waste any more time with her.

VII. Investigate her background. Question the nanny's references carefully, and if she is not agency-screened, get a professional to check out police, court, credit, and driving records for signs of trouble.

VIII. See how she is in practice. Always try to arrange at least a day or two of "try-out" babysitting, while you stay at home, so that you can see for yourself if you are pleased.

IX. Be accommodating in areas where negotiation is possible. You don't want to lose out on a good nanny because you failed to reach agreement about something relatively minor, such as whether Presidents' Day is a holiday.

X. Stress the importance of good communication. If both of you do your best to be honest and considerate of the other, you will be able to work out any difficulties that crop up, and you will go on to build a good, long-term relationship.

The Nannies Get Their Say

All the focus up to now has been on finding a nanny that suits your needs. In my research for this book I talked to many nannies, too. I have saved till the end some of their reflections on the topic of nanny-employer relations. After looking over my interview notes, I have compiled a top-ten list of nannies' most common complaints about parents, which are as follows:

1. **Lack of candor upon hiring.** Parents don't reveal all the relevant facts about the job (e.g., their little boy is a biter, or they expect the nanny to clean the house).

2. **Low pay.** Employers seldom pay what a good nanny deserves to earn.

3. **Overtime.** Parents want lots of extra hours, and usually for the same rate of pay, and without sufficient notice.

4. **No support for the nanny's authority.** Parents barge in when the nanny has just told the child something, and they say just the opposite.

5. **Lack of scheduling courtesy.** Parents don't consult the nanny about scheduling changes, family vacations, or trips the nanny is expected to take with the family.

6. **Lack of appreciation.** Parents take the nanny for granted, never taking the time to write a note of appreciation, or even say thank you.

7. **Meddling.** Parents interfere in her private life, asking too many intrusive questions and giving her unsolicited advice.

8. **Restrictions.** Parents treat her like a child, telling her what time she must be in, and attempting to control what she does on her days off.

9. **Inconsistency.** Parents tell her to respond to a child's problem in a certain way, and the next time she does so, they say, "No, not that way," telling her to take a completely different approach.

10. **Blame.** Anything that goes wrong, the parents assume it's the nanny's fault. They never wait to hear her side of the story.

The Safe Nanny Checklist

When you've found a nanny who can be accurately described by each one of the statements below, you can be sure you have a safe one.

❑ She meets my stated minimum requirements: She will work the hours I need, for the pay I'm offering, and she has the specific skills I'm looking for (e.g., driving, cooking, homework supervision).

❑ She appears to be stable, emotionally mature, and professional in outlook.

❑ She appears enthusiastic about working for me and my family.

❑ She has the necessary training and experience to do the job.

❑ She has the physical capability to perform the duties I require.

❑ She is CPR certified (or she is willing to complete a CPR course within a set interval after hiring).

❑ Her references have confirmed her childcare skills and praised her reliability and good judgment.

❑ She has completed at least one practice baby-sitting session under my supervision and performed to my satisfaction.

❑ She is attentive to my instructions and is a quick study about the way I like things done.

❑ She is safety-conscious, familiar with most safety rules, child-proofing devices, and emergency procedures.

❑ I have no particular qualms, misgivings, or uneasy feelings about hiring this nanny.

❑ I have been able to settle with her any negotiable issues she raised about provisions in the Employment Agreement (and/or the Live-in Agreement).

❑ I like her, and I get the feeling I will enjoy having her around.

If your nanny candidate gets a checkmark in every box, congratulations! You've got a great one. If you are hesitant about checking off two or more boxes, it may be time to start posting the notices again, or call the agency back. You never want to leave your children with someone about whom you have doubts.

Some Final Thoughts About the Childcare Problem in America Today—and Some Possible Solutions

It wasn't supposed to be this hard. In a country with as many people as ours, people who are, by and large, hard-working, well-educated, and caring, you might expect that there would be an oversupply of young people willing and qualified to look after the children of working parents. But we parents who have been out there looking know that it's just not so.

We also know that in many other countries there is no such shortage. We know that from points all around the globe there are many young women (and a few young men) who are eager for the opportunity to come to the United States and take childcare jobs for a short time, or even as a permanent career choice. Right now the only way for these people to emigrate legally is to find an employer willing to wait the eight to ten years it takes for a sponsored worker to be approved to receive a "green card" under current immigration rules. Needless to say, only a handful of parents can afford to wait that long for a nanny.

The only program that exists now to bring foreign childcare workers to this country is the au pair program that is part of the U.S. Information Agency—but it is set up to function more as a cultural exchange experience for the benefit of young Europeans than as a source of competent, professional childcare for American families. Without a doubt, the au pair program has caused more problems than it has solved: problems of unmet expectations on both sides, of underpaid and exploited young women, and dissatisfied parents with inadequately supervised children.

Reform is sorely needed. The first and most obvious step would be to abandon the pretense that au pairs are here as exchange students. Overseas recruiters should make clear that workers are being sought as full-time childcare professionals. Minimum standards should be instituted to ensure that candidates are experienced and capable of performing the job required. A full-scale childcare training course should be a prerequisite—not just a few hours of class time, as is now the case. Most important, oversight of the program should be moved from the USIA to the U.S. Department of Labor.

To answer critics who charge that a foreign nanny recruitment program would take jobs away from qualified Americans, the Labor Department should survey parents and job-hunting nannies to assess the situation region by region. Applications by parents to bring over nannies could be restricted to those who live in regions in which the labor shortage has been demonstrated to be most severe.

Another important reform concerns the time limitation in place for au pairs. The current one-year limit is just the wrong amount of time for most families: It is just long enough for a small child to begin to form a strong emotional bond with a nanny, and then it's over. Three to five years would make far more sense for both caregivers and families.

Broadening the bases for recruitment is another idea that deserves exploration. The au pair program as it operates today draws mainly from the countries of western Europe, largely ignoring countries in eastern Europe and Asia, many of which have high unemployment rates among young women with professional training as teachers, nurses, or as members of other childcare-related fields. Many of these well-educated workers would emigrate to the United States if they knew they could find work legally as nannies.

Periodically, the U.S. Immigration and Naturalization Service operates a green-card lottery in certain countries. The only way under the law, as it stands, for foreign childcare workers to have a chance for permission to immigrate is to put their names in the hat and hope for the best. Changes in our immigration laws could give preference to immigrants who can provide skills and services that are in certifiably short supply. Immigrants who have a particular skill to contribute and who are enthusiastic about their work tend to make excellent, hard-working citizens, contributing to our economy far more than they receive. It makes good sense all around (not just for parents of small children) to seek such people out actively—not leaving it to the luck of the draw.

Increasing the supply of qualified caregivers is all to the good, but on the other side of the ledger, much needs to be done to help parents who are unable to afford the high quality of care that all children deserve. The current tax structure provides a childcare credit that barely makes a dent in the average family's childcare costs. The point needs to be brought home to all Americans (not just parents) that it benefits the whole of society to have our nations' children kept in safe, competent hands. Put the other way, we all suffer when the next generation is badly brought up, alienated, and insecure.

Some people oppose a national underwriting of childcare costs because they believe that it discourages mothers from staying home with their children. These critics are living in the past. Women have learned from the bitter experiences of their mothers and grandmothers that it is too risky to become dependent on the male partner for a lifetime of support. They have seen that their safest choice in life is to acquire a skill or enter a profession and not abandon their earning potential during their childbearing years. The alternative could well be to end up divorced or widowed, with no prospect of contributing to the economy and no way to pay for all the things their children need. That isn't to the benefit of mothers, children, or society as a whole.

For nearly two decades now, working mothers have been in the majority, even those with children under school age. One might assume that we, as women, would have the political clout by now to make legislatures recognize our plight and give us the support that both we and society deeply need. The trouble is, most of us are too timid to take a stand. All too often we are riddled with ambivalent feelings about our place in the workforce, and guilt-ridden each time we kiss our children good-bye. We wonder if we are really capable of doing our best, both on the job and in the home—though we seldom ask the children's fathers the same hard question. We keep looking at ourselves and our families as unique cases—we haven't developed the habit of addressing the issue collectively. So we don't fight collectively for the childcare subsidy that we need.

It's my hope that this book will be of use to many individual families in finding a high level of childcare for their children. It's my hope with this short essay to spur some of you on to join in the political fight that will make it possible for millions more of our children to receive that same high level of care. Of course, to have a little time leftover to devote to a cause, you do need to have a great nanny looking after your kids. So take care of that first—and good luck to you in your search!

EMPLOYMENT AGREEMENT
[Sample]

[Fill in the blanks according to the terms you and your nanny have negotiated. Alter the language in paragraphs on Health Insurance, Vacations, Days Off, and other benefits as needed to reflect your employment package. Check Chapter Five for any other issues, such as Non-childcare Duties, that you wish to cover in your Employment Agreement.]

This Agreement is between_____, Nanny, and _____, Employers, for nanny services starting on _____[date] at_____ _____[address of your house].

Regular schedule. Nanny will work _____ hours per week, _____ through _____, from _____ A.M. to _____ P.M.

Salary. Nanny will be paid $_____ per week, to be paid on _____ for the week preceding.

Overtime. Hours in excess of _____ per week will be compensated at a rate of $_____ per hour, unless an overnight stay is required. Payment for childcare for 24 or more continuous hours and/or involving overnight travel will be arranged on an ad hoc basis, and is not part of this Agreement.

Health Insurance. After completion of the Trial Period, Nanny may subscribe to the health insurance plan offered by Employers. The monthly premium of $_____ is to be paid _____% by Nanny and _____% by Employers. If Nanny chooses not to enroll in Employer-provided health insurance, she may accept $10 per week additional in salary, to be used to purchase a health insurance policy of her choice. Nanny's initials here _____ serve as her waiver of Employer-provided health insurance.

Vacations. After Nanny has worked for Employers for a period of six months, she is entitled to five paid vacation days. For each subsequent six-month period she works, she earns another five days of paid vacation. Paid vacation days do not accumulate beyond one year. Nanny must provide one month's notice of her intention to use her paid vacation days.

Other days off. Paid holidays are: Labor Day, Thanksgiving, Christmas, New Year's Day, Martin Luther King's Birthday, Memorial Day, and Independence Day.

Sick Days. Nanny will be paid for up to five days not worked due to illness.

Unpaid leave. Nanny may take up to five days leave without pay in the event of a family emergency. Such leave is not automatic but must be requested with as much advance notice to Employers as possible. Employers will make reasonable efforts to accommodate Nanny's need for time off, but cannot guarantee that unpaid leave will be granted.

Duties. Nanny will provide childcare for _____ [child or children's names], including straightening up their rooms, preparing their meals, cleaning up after their meals, doing their laundry, giving them baths, playing with them, reading to them, arranging outings, and performing other tasks necessary to ensure their health, safety, and well-being.

Trial period. The first _____ days after the starting date of this Agreement constitute the Trial Period. During the Trial Period the Employers shall arrange for Nanny to become certified in CPR and provide other safety and childcare training necessary for the job. Within the Trial Period either Nanny or employers may terminate this agreement without notice, severance pay, penalty, or explanation.

Termination of employment by Nanny. Once the Trial Period has ended, Nanny agrees to provide a minimum of _____ weeks notice of her intention to quit her employment.

Termination of employment by Employer. In the event that her employment is terminated after the Trial Period has ended, Nanny will be entitled to two weeks' severance pay in lieu of two weeks' notice, provided that termination is not due to any criminal misconduct or negligence on Nanny's part.

Renewal of this Agreement. This Agreement will automatically renew on the anniversary of its starting date, unless terminated as described in any of the three preceding paragraphs.

Modifications. Both Nanny and Employers must agree to any modifications, which shall be written into this agreement in the appropriate section and initialed and dated by all parties. Modifications to this agreement will renew at the same time the entire agreement renews.

signed:

_____ _____   _____ _____

Nanny   Date   Employer   Date

                                                    _____ _____

                                                    Employer   Date

LIVE-IN AGREEMENT
[Sample]

[Fill in the blanks or alter the language in the paragraphs below as necessary to describe your particular live-in accommodations. You may want to add paragraphs to cover noise policies, TV viewing policies, health club membership policies, or any other particular house rules you wish to impose. See Chapter Five for suggestions of issues to be included.]

This Agreement between _____, Nanny, and _____, Employers, lays out the terms under which Nanny may occupy a _____ [room, live-in suite, basement apartment] at _____ [your home address].

Employers will provide Nanny with room and board while she is employed taking care of _____ [name of child or children]. Nanny is not considered a tenant, nor are Employers to be considered her landlords.

Furnishings. Live-in accommodations include: a bed, a dresser, a nightstand, a bookcase, an armchair, a rug, a Sony TV, a Panasonic VCR, an Aiwa CD/tape player, a standing halogen lamp, a table lamp, a Sharp microwave, a Kenmore mini-refrigerator, a Mr. Coffee coffeemaker, and a GE toaster oven. These items belong to Employers and may not be removed from the premises for any reason without the express permission of Employers.

Responsibility for damages. Nanny agrees to be responsible for keeping the room neat and clean. If any damage should occur to the room either through negligence or misconduct on the part of Nanny or her guests, Nanny bears full responsibility for repairs. If cost of repairs exceeds $_____, Employers may deduct _____ percent from Nanny's salary each week until the full amount is reimbursed.

Alterations. Nanny must obtain permission of Employers before making any alterations to the room. She may not change paint colors, remove or install wallpaper, attach any fixtures to walls, drill any holes or make any other permanent changes without first receiving permission from Employers.

Repairs. Should any appliance, plumbing fixture, lighting fixture, part of heating/cooling system or any other part of the room need repair, Nanny is obligated to report the problem to Employers without delay and permit Employers' authorized workmen to have access to the room to effect needed repairs.

Telephone. Employers will have a telephone line installed at their expense in Nanny's room and will pay the monthly service charge of _____. Nanny will be responsible for paying for all long-distance calls she makes from her telephone or from any other telephone in the house, except for calls made at the specific request of Employers.

Keys. Nanny is provided with two sets of keys. If locks to the house need to be changed because Nanny has lost keys or given keys out without Employers' authorization, Nanny will be responsible for the cost of the change.

Trial Period. Nanny and Employer each have _____ days to decide if the live-in employment arrangement is satisfactory. Within that time either party may terminate the arrangement without notice, explanation, or penalty. Nanny must move out of Employers' home within _____ days of termination of employment during the Trial Period. Because it may not be possible to secure a new residence on such limited notice, Nanny must make arrangements for a back-up place to stay in case of termination during the Trial Period.

Termination after the end of the Trial Period. Nanny has _____ days to move out when employment is terminated after the end of the Trial Period.

Guest policy. Nanny must seek permission from Employers to have an overnight guest for more than _____ nights. Nanny's overnight guests are to be accommodated in her room, with a one-week maximum stay.

signed:

_____	_____	_____	_____
Nanny	Date	Employer	Date

_____	_____
Employer	Date

APPENDIX C

AUTHORIZATION TO SEARCH RECORDS
[Sample]

I, _____, applicant for the position of Nanny at _____ [your home address] hereby authorize _____ [employers' names] or their designated agent to investigate my background in the following areas: criminal records, civil court records, motor vehicle records, credit records, employment history, and any other areas relevant to my character or suitability for employment in a childcare position. This authorization is not limited to records held in any state or jurisdiction. I agree to hold _____ [employers' names] harmless for any effects such search may have on my ability to obtain work now or at any time in the future.

signed:

_____ _____
Applicant   Date

RESOURCE GUIDE

On-line Resources

The Internet is a treasure trove of information for parents and nannies alike. After just a few hours of net-surfing I uncovered over 200 websites of interest, including listings for:

- national nanny agencies
- international nanny agencies
- nanny schools
- nanny tax assistance
- nanny background checkers
- nanny video surveillance companies
- nanny support groups
- nanny product sales
- nanny tips
- nanny to nanny chat groups
- parent to parent chat groups
- parent to nanny chat groups
- child health and safety information
- child development information

Rather than attempt to compile a lengthy list of all the relevant websites, I have chosen three general-interest nanny websites, each of which has its own list of "links" to many other websites. The Internet user may then click on the link of interest and jump directly to that site. The fourth website listed below is that of the U.S. Consumer Product Safety Commission, which gives parents access to the latest information on unsafe toys and baby products.

Christine Maniscalco's Life with Nanny Website
www.atmavidya.com/lifewithnanny

This is a multifeatured, easy-to-navigate website, full of information about all aspects of parent-nanny relationships. It even includes rainy-day projects and children's artwork onscreen. The "Links" listing section provides a mini-description of what sort of information you will find on each link, so that you don't waste time visiting sites that are not relevant to your interests.

HomeWork Solutions
www.nannynetwork.com/

Anyone searching the web who types the word "nanny" into a search engine is sure to end up at this very complete and useful website. Especially helpful for those who will be handling their own nanny-tax paperwork is the page that walks you through the calculation of payroll taxes. You can also contact HomeWork Solutions through their toll-free number to sign up for their fee-based service that takes care of the paperwork for you.

I Love My Nanny Network
www.ilovemynanny.com/

This website lists nanny support groups state by state, sells nanny books and products, has a nanny qualifications form that you can download and print for use during the candidate evaluation process, and publishes a newsletter called the *I Love My Nanny News*.

The U.S. Consumer Product Safety Commission
www.cpsc.gov

The quickest way to find out about recalls of toys or baby equipment is to access this site and click on "recalls," and "categorized by topic." Another helpful section of the website is called "4 Kids," and is written at the reading level of a child age eight or older. Kids can learn about safety on the playground, on bikes, on in-line skates, on skateboards, and while playing team sports such as baseball or football. There is also a section that teaches older kids how to become safe, effective babysitters themselves.

To Obtain Nanny Health or Life Insurance

Richard E. Eisenberg, CLU, CHFC
Insurance for Nannies
1340 Centre Street, Suite 203
Newton, MA 02159
1-800-777-5765

For Help in Figuring Nanny Taxes

HomeWork Solutions
Nanitax Service
2 Pidgeon Hill Drive, Suite 210
Sterling, VA 20165
1-703-404-8151

Safety and Baby-Proofing Products

The catalogs listed below specialize in products to keep your home and family safe. Call the toll-free number to receive a catalog, featuring items recommended in this book, such as carbon monoxide monitors; folding fire escape ladders; flood detectors; furniture edge protectors and bumpers; baby-gates; cabinet locks and latches; carseats and boosters; and much, much more.

The Safety Zone	1-800-999-3030
Perfectly Safe	1-800-837-KIDS
Masune First Aid and Safety	1-800-831-0894
One Step Ahead	1-800-274-8440
The Right Start	1-800-LITTLE-1

INDEX

The Safe Nanny Handbook

Also by P E G G Y R O B I N

Bottle-Feeding Without Guilt

How to Be a Successful Fertility Patient

Outwitting Toddlers (with Bill Adler, Jr.)

Saving the Neighborhood